Testimonials

MW01104935

"As an accountant and fraud information about financial processes, particularly complex financial processes that are frequently abused by unscrupulous "advisors." *UnMasking the Mortgage Madness* is written to reach all audiences with an easy, conversational style that arms the reader with a powerful and liberating understanding of the mortgage process."

—Tony Yuenger, CPA, CFE, CIA
Gig Harbor, Washington

"Anybody with plans to purchase a home or refinance, has simply GOT to read this book. Rick Bulman boils down the complicated mortgage process, to something every one of us can understand. And more importantly, I feel like I am armed with the knowledge I need to go into my next home purchase, as an educated consumer. Thank you Rick for providing the nuts and bolts. You have simplified the 'Mortgage Madness' once and for all!"

—Carleen Bohannon
News Anchor/Reporter
Seattle, Washington

"Rick Bulman has accomplished what many loan officers have tried to do with their clients. He has taken a complex subject matter and simplified it for the layman. Through real life stories coupled with humor and practical application, *UnMasking the Mortgage Madness*, is a fun easy read. This book will keep you going from chapter to chapter. It's industry insight that proves to be a must read for any current or potential homeowner!"

—Jon Magill, President/CEO
PMAC Bank, Chino Hills, CA

"Integrity, Honesty, and Value — not only is this book enlightening, it is a must read for anyone seeking to finance a home. Rick has unleashed the secret for combining humor and story telling into what normally would make for a pretty dry read. He has opened the door to a whole new level for the mortgage industry and the way they should do business."

—Lora L. Mullins
Co-Founder and EVP
Corporate Performance Group

"*UnMasking the Mortgage Madness* is a must read for all real estate agents that don't understand the issues and the complexities of this business that we are so intertwined with. The information that Rick gives will help agents have smoother closings by enabling them to better prepare themselves, their clients and all of those involved in the transaction and be ahead of any potential transaction disasters. I recommend anyone to take the time to educate themselves through *UnMasking the Mortgage Madness.*"

—Jim Perry, Real Estate Agent
RE/MAX Professionals

"As a Financial Advisor, I am always looking for ways to help my clients make well informed decisions. *UnMasking the Mortgage Madness* is a powerful tool that levels the playing field. Rick Bulman's message sets a new standard of integrity for the lending industry to follow. Keep up the good work!"

—Dan Driscoll, Financial Advisor
Brookstreet Securities Corporation
Brea, California

"*UnMasking the Mortgage Madness* is a must-read for anyone who sincerely wants to understand and better manage the loan process. Rick offers very practical tips for ensuring you are receiving the fairest rates and fees possible — all in an easy to read, conversational style. What makes the book most enduring is Rick's genuine interest in empowering and educating others so they can obtain the best mortgages in their loan process. Bravo!"

—Lisa Kopp, CFA
Director, Strategic Infrastructure
Russell Investment Group

"This is a fresh, innovative book with great information that will help any client save money. *UnMasking the Mortgage Madness* clearly communicates through the process, from the first-time home-buyer to the seasoned investor, whether buying or refinancing."

—Newton Bruington, Owner
Green Lake Mortgage

"This book is an exciting and engaging read. Rick's skill as a storyteller coupled with his insight into the mortgage industry bring to life concepts otherwise academic. Rick's instruction allows the layperson to negotiate the mortgage process with the confidence of a professional. Rick has saved my family thousands of dollars through both a purchase and a refinance as he guided us through the steps he outlines in his book. *UnMasking the Mortgage Madness* is a must read for anyone looking to purchase or refinance a home."

— Reverend Jon McIntosh
Senior Pastor, Grace Church
Federal Way, Washington

"*Unmasking The Mortgage Madness* has really opened my eyes and helped me to understand the mortgage process. As a homeowner myself, having had two home loans and being a Real Estate Agent, I still had no idea what fees and figures a loan entailed or that my clients could have been victims of predatory lending. Having known the facts and information this book offers BEFORE buying a home could have saved my prior clients and me a lot of money. Knowledge is key. This book is a must read for anyone thinking of buying a home or any Real Estate Agent who has not been educated thoroughly in the mortgage business. I am so thankful, and my future clients will be too!"

—Laura Stockler, Real Estate Agent
Real Estate USA

"As a long-time real estate investor, I have long looked for anything at all that would give me an advantage, some way to save a buck here or a buck there. *UnMasking the Mortgage Madness* pays off in spades. The very first exposure I had to the information provided in the book enabled me to save a close friend hundreds of dollars. He was in the process of acquiring a mortgage and he, like many others, was under the impression that line items on a Good Faith Estimate were fixed and non-negotiable. As he read some numbers to me from his Good Faith Estimate, there were several items that simply did not sound right. I read him some excerpts from the book, and the next day he called me to say he used that information to save himself a substantial amount of money. Whether you are going through the process of buying a home now or will be doing it in the future, *UnMasking the Mortgage Madness* is a book well worth reading. Rick Bulman does a great job of breaking down the process into easy-to-understand language and keeps it real. You will not be disappointed."

—Stephen M. John
Vice President, Sales (retired)
Magnolia Audio-Video
A Subsidiary of Best Buy Co.

"I was given incredible information through *UnMasking the Mortgage Madness*. In past years, I have found myself overwhelmed with all the voices and choices thrown at us regarding real estate, mortgage financing, etc. I have often wondered if there could be a standard of information provided to the "lay" buyer to gain a better understanding of this type of financing. The information in *UnMasking the Mortgage Madness* is truly an eye-opener."

—Jim and Sally Huffey, Homeowner
Eau Claire, Wisconsin

"*UnMasking the Mortgage Madness* gives you a glimpse into what is often a confusing process for the consumer. As we went through the closing process of our last home, we just hoped that we could trust the mortgage company. If we had an opportunity to educate ourselves through something like *UnMasking the Mortgage Madness*, we could have purchased our home with 100% confidence by, knowing our loan officer had our best interest in mind."

—Jay and Whitney Brain, Homeowner
Frederick, Maryland

"I have been empowered by the *UnMasking the Mortgage Madness* presentation. Rick has revealed certain aspects of the typical loan development that changed my perspective of the process. I am equipped to ask the right questions the right way to ensure that I can get the best rate for my situation, while providing adequate compensation for the representative who is working the loan for me. Now, I can make better decisions."

—Clint Byington, Homeowner
Livermore, California

"I have bought many homes in my lifetime. What I have learned through *UnMasking the Mortgage Madness* would have been helpful for me to know. I never knew to request such documents such as a lock confirmation sheet. The knowledge I have gained through the information Rick Bulman has provided turned my loan transaction from a stressful experience into a peaceful one. I feel more in control Thank you!"

—Tony Drago, Homeowner
Las Vegas, Nevada

"My husband and I have moved sixteen times, so house buying is something that comes easy to me, until it comes to all the loan documents — papers, papers, papers. I usually just sit back, pretend I know what everyone is talking about, and go off somewhere thinking about colors, furniture, and curtains. I did this because I never understood what was being said, even when it was explained to me. I felt like a visitor in a foreign land. After reading Rick Bulman's book, I have a better understanding of what words mean and why things are being done. I shudder to think of all the homes we've bought in the past and been taken advantage of. Thanks, Rick, you've helped prepare me for this year's summer move."

—Sharré Fox, Homeowner
Real Estate Investor
Auburn, Washington

"*UnMasking the Mortgage Madness* is sure to become an industry staple for those who are trying to teach mortgage concepts. With 17 years in the mortgage field, I have never encountered a book that simplifies our field the way that this book does. Rick Bulman's knowledgeable insights will empower consumers and aspiring professionals alike. Thank you, Rick, for all your hard work! My clients and students will be thanking you for years to come."

—John Driscoll, Sr. Vice President
Mortgage Planner & Trainer
PMAC University, Chino Hills, CA

"As a title and escrow sales consultant, I work with numerous agents and lenders. About six years ago I received a phone call from Rick Bulman. That was the beginning of a very exciting business relationship. Rick's *UnMasking the Mortgage Madness* has brought considerable value to our real estate market. No bells and whistles, just the plain truth about the mortgage business. I highly recommend this book to anyone who wants to do it right the first time."

—Tobi Snider
First American Title and Escrow

UnMasking the Mortgage Madness

by

Rick Bulman

Library of Congress Control Number: 2007926298
Printed in the United States of America

Quantities of this book are available at a volume discount.
For more information visit: www.rickbulman.com

Editing: Cherie Tucker
Cover Design & Interior Layout: William E. G. Johnson
Photography: Christopher Conrad

Note: All loan programs, interest rates, and underwriting guidelines
are volatile in nature and subject to change. Examples discussed in
this book are for illustrative purposes and reference only. All consumers should consult with their local mortgage professional for the most
recent loan programs, interest rates, and underwriting guidelines.

This publication is designed to provide accurate and authoritative information
in regard to the subject matter covered. It is sold with the understanding
that the publisher is not engaged in rendering legal, accounting, or other
professional advice. If legal advice or other expert assistance is required,
the services of a competent professional person should be sought.

Permission granted for all forms utilized by
PMAC Lending Services and Calyx Point

Classic Day Publishing LLC
2925 Fairview Ave E.
Seattle, WA 98102
877.728.8837
www.peanutbutterpublishing.com
info@peanutbutterpublishing.com

This
book is
dedicated to
the five most impor-
tant people to me: My wife,
Tiffany, who is my best friend, my
companion, my helpmate. I could not
think of a better person to spend this
journey of life with. Thank you for saying
Yes to me! My three boys Kaleb, Joshua,
and Jared. You are my three little men.
When I see you, I see me. You all make
me laugh and make living life so worth
it. You are going to grow to be great men!
My daughter, Faith. You are so precious
to daddy. You will always be my little
girl. You will always be my Ta Da! You
melt my heart with your hugs and kisses.

CONTENTS

Acknowledgments

It is a pleasure to thank several individuals who have helped shaped this book through their encouragement, support, and advice.

To my beautiful and supportive wife, Tiffany. I appreciate your patience and encouragement as I've championed this project. Thank you for believing in me, and allowing me to work late into multiple nights typing away in our bedroom. Your support speaks volumes to me, as you had to put up with the light from my lap top screen and the constant pecking of my keyboard while you were trying to sleep. You are wonderful! I love you!

To my four beautiful children: Kaleb, Joshua, Jared, and Faith. Thank you for being patient with me. No more being quiet when you come upstairs. Now, you can be as loud as you want.

To my parents and in-laws: Rick and Kathi Bulman, Tony Drago, and Jerry and Sharré Fox. Your support and encouraging words mean the world to me. I love you and thank you for believing in the cause I am passionate about.

To Steve John: I value our friendship. Thank you for partnering with me on so many different levels. Your wisdom and advice I cherish! You have literally help make this possible!

To Elliott Wolf: Thank you for taking on this project. Your help and direction is extremely appreciated. Thank you for believing in this book, the cause, and in me.

To Steve and Jennifer McConnell, Jeff and Stephanie Endsley, and Joe and Kari Bulman: Your love and support for this book project has been felt and cherished. I love you all.

To Steve McConnell: Your partnership in the *UnMasking the Mortgage Madness* project (video, web, and book) is greatly appreciated and valued. You are a needed and a valued asset. Thank you for your professionalism and faith in the very cause of this venture.

To Jay and Whitney Brain, Mike Stath, Lora Mullins, Keri Mattison, and Tony Yuenger for your encouragement and support in writing what will hopefully empower many people when dealing with lenders. You all are loved and appreciated.

To Jon McIntosh, or should I call you Mr. Lentz: Thank you for always taking my calls at 10:30 at night to help me process some of the craziness that goes into such a project. You are a great friend with great wisdom. In some ways, *your words have impacted this book*. Thank you!

To Dan Driscoll, Peter Assad, and Newton Bruington who read major portions of the manuscript and made important and much appreciated suggestions. I've appreciated your honesty, your input, and support. Your professionalism and knowledge are valued.

To my colleagues who have supported such a project with encouraging words and advice: John Driscoll, Jon Magill, Katie Emory, Tina Timbang, Sandy Neeper (*great processor*) and Tobi Snider (*great title rep*). You all are very much appreciated. I thank you.

To PMAC Lending Services: Jon, you and your staff have been very helpful. Thank you for allowing the utilization of your disclosure forms. Your support is greatly appreciated.

To Calyx Point: Thank you for the utilization of your forms.

To John Schneider: Thank you for writing the forward to this book. Your friendship and support have meant a lot. Thank you for partnering with me in this way!

To Cherie Tucker: Thank you for your wisdom that was poured out to me in red ink.

To William Johnson: I do not know of a more talented individual. Every project you do for me you hit out of the park. Once again, with the design of this book you have nailed it. Your future is beyond bright. You are a great gift. Thank you!

Thank you to everyone who took time to write such wonderful words on my behalf in the testimonial section of this book. Your advocacy is greatly appreciated.

Most importantly, thank you, Lord, for the strength and creativity to produce such a book.

Foreword

I t seems as though every day there is some new twist being offered up to the public with regard to home mortgages or refinancing offers. Turn on any radio, open any newspaper, or just turn on the television. They are always coming at you, and it seems as though you cannot escape. The best you can hope for is to develop some paranormal ability to tune it all out. The noise around mortgages is deafening. Between the overwhelming number of traditional lenders and the glut of special offers from your friendly independent mortgage broker, the input overload can be truly maddening.

For those of us who tread cautiously into the world of home mortgages out of need, it also seems that taking on such a topic in a book is tantamount to foolish bravery. However, I have known Rick Bulman for a number of years, and I know that he is neither foolish nor does he have to be brave in taking on this task. He is well qualified to guide us through this maze. A deep understanding of the subject matter and needs of the typical homeowner is what makes his sensible, plain-talk approach to understanding mortgages unique. This understanding is enriched by a sensitivity to the plight of the average head of the household, who must wade through the vast sea of confusing and often misleading offers, then decide what can and cannot be believed before making an informed decision.

This book is written from the perspective of one who has spent much energy thinking about the impact of the sheer weight of information bombarding the average single-family dweller. Rick's commitment to dispelling myths and exposing half-truths is worth the price of the book by itself. I am comforted by the knowledge that this book is written by someone whose periscope has been focused primarily, if not solely, on home mortgages and refinancing.

Four things made this book particularly useful for me. First, it simplifies the industry jargon and promotional hyperbole down to easy-to-understand concepts. Many homeowners have suffered the consequences of acting on limited or invalid understandings of extremely complex sets of numbers and multitudes of confusing forms. Quite simply, Rick tells you which forms need your utmost attention and what numbers are most easily negotiated into savings.

Second, every aspect of this book is based on the distinction between puffery and fact. This distinction is a difficult one to make for many who are not well versed in the language spoken by some competitive lending institutions, many of whom are not beyond a little misdirection in an attempt to hide some unnecessary charges. In his casual and story-telling way, the author helps us understand not only the importance of these distinctions but their essence.

Third, this book provides us with samples, tools for producing, interpreting, and reporting reliable data required for effective decision making.

Finally, this book makes the solid relationship between the mortgage broker and the homeowner one of the primary factors in the decision making process. Rick does not teach you to catch mistakes and to drive a wedge through that relationship with confrontation. Instead, he teaches you to walk into a relationship armed with an understanding of and comfort level with the subject matter, then to use the power that comes with that knowledge to build a solid relationship with your broker. I cannot emphasize enough how important this is.

In my long television career, the bulk of my energies have been spent on becoming better at my trade and devoted to raising a family. I have certainly not spent a great deal of time trying to understand the ins and outs of the mortgage business. Yet, for most of us, a home will be one of the largest and most important investments of our lives. Failure to really understand the very best option with regard to a mortgage could be an incredibly costly mistake.

With *UnMasking the Mortgage Madness* Rick Bulman arms us with everything we need to know about the different options and provides us with valuable insights into ways to save money. I know that as a homeowner and investor, when I have the opportunity to engage in future real estate transactions, I'll have this book handy to use as a guide.

Enjoy!

John Schneider
Dukes of Hazzard
Smallville
Real Estate Investor

Introduction

When I was in high school I liked Algebra. Don't get me wrong – I hated math like most other kids, but the class was great because I had a great teacher. He was able to make the complexities of math simple and understandable. He was as concerned with the process as he was with the outcome and took time to answer my questions without making me feel foolish for having them. I remember one day I was getting frustrated and just gave up. He saw the frustration in me and wanted to help, but I refused. I just wanted the class to end and to go on with my day. However, I can still recall what he said as I was throwing in the towel. "I understand your frustration. I hate not knowing something. It drives me nuts." I had a moment of self-realization that day. I hate not knowing something. When things are unclear or confusing, it drives me crazy!

There are many things in life that are that way for me. Planes, for instance. The engineering that goes into their design is a mystery. When I was 21 years old, my friend Adam was licensed to fly twin-engine airplanes. He asked me if my wife, Tiffany, and I would like to go up with him. I still remember we had to pool our money together to rent a small four-seater plane for the hour. We took off together, and at 12,000 feet it suddenly occurred to me the oldest person in the plane was only twenty-three and had quit flight school to pursue a different career. It was a sobering thought to realize that our lives were in the hands of an inexperienced pilot whose qualifications were in question.

All of a sudden my inability to control my own environ-ment made me very uncomfortable. The only way to rid myself of that discomfort would be to regain some measure of control, but I wasn't qualified either. So, genius that I am, I asked Adam if I could fly the plane! Genius that he was, he let me! I don't think my wife was very pleased. I sat in the seat next to him. The panel in front of me had its own set of controls. Adam began to walk me through the features of the plane. He started off talking about the plane's attitude. He began to share that the plane must have a level attitude, as he pointed to a dial (attitude indicator) that had the picture of the horizon at the top and the ground on the bottom. He said if he were to pull the plane upward, it would have a nose-high attitude, which by the way, could cut the engine off. If he pointed the nose downward, then the plane would have a nose-down attitude. He went on to point out the pedals and what their functions were. He dem-onstrated the pedals and the steering and then the moment I was waiting for. He said, "Try to keep the plane's attitude level and have fun." Of course, he was there the whole time and would explain what to do and what not to do. He talked me through the plane's design and each instrument's purpose and function, explaining the theory of flight and how to stay safe in the sky.

As soon as I understood the "how and why" behind fly-ing, I was able to relax and enjoy myself. Of course, know-ing I had a co-pilot to step in if things got dangerous was a big help too. Understanding the process and having a coach who was willing to work with me made all the difference.

The mortgage industry is no different for many people. It's a completely foreign process we enter into with little or no information, relying on a "pilot" to get us safely to our destination (and hoping that he or she is actually qualified). Perhaps the thought of getting a mortgage makes you a little uneasy. Perhaps you are uncertain which of the many mortgage types is right for you. Maybe you have heard *horror stories* from friends or family members that make you question the integrity of the process. Getting a mortgage can be intimidating for the uninformed purchaser. If your loan agent will take the time to explain what to expect and when to expect it and answer your questions along the way, you can actually walk through a home financing experience with peace and confidence.

People need a mortgage for a number of reasons. They may be first-time homebuyers, or they may be upgrading and moving into something larger. They may be empty nesters looking to downsize. Perhaps they are investors purchasing new properties or current homeowners refinancing a mortgage to pay off debt, make home improvements, or simply lower their interest rate for a more manageable payment. Regardless of the reason for obtaining a mortgage, they all will work with a loan agent to accomplish their objective. If you were to line up 100 of these people who went through the mortgage process, it would be safe to say more than 60 percent of them paid more than what they should have in closing costs. Out of a random 953 loans that I personally reviewed, 588 of those clients paid higher closing costs than they needed to pay. That's 62 percent! If I had to guess, you would rather be part of the 38 percent who paid a fair and just price for a loan agent's services.

How can you know for sure that you are getting a good deal? How do you know you are seeing all the fees in the loan? Do you know what fees to look out for? Is your interest rate truly the lowest rate available? I would even go so far as to say that nine times out of ten the interest rate sold by the loan agent is not the lowest rate available. It is not uncommon to find that there was a rate .250 to .500% lower. I will show you how to safeguard yourself against this kind of thing.

As a Mortgage Banker, I have seen some very aggressive predatory lending. Take "Beth" for example. "Beth" is an elderly woman in Kent, Washington. Back when cold calling was the way to get business, I contacted her only days before she was due to sign her loan documents with another banker. She said she was having second thoughts about signing because she was worried her interest rate and fees were too high. I asked her what they were, and to my surprise her rate was .750% higher than what she qualified for and, although her loan amount was only $250,000, they were charging her an origination fee of $9,000! Do you know what an increase of .750% in your interest rate translates to over the course of a 30-year loan? A loan amount of $250,000 with an interest rate of 7.75% would give Beth a monthly payment of $1,791. With a .750% lower interest rate, at 7 percent, that would give her a monthly payment of $1,663. That is a $128 a month payment difference. That difference translates to $1,533 per year of excess spending.

If she kept the loan for 30-years, she would have overspent, through her higher interest rate, $46,080. If she kept the loan only for ten years, she still would have overspent, through her higher interest rate, $15,360. I begged her to stop! Not because I needed her business, but because I felt as if a crime was taking place and she was the victim.

When a person falls in to predatory lending it gives mortgage banking a bad name. Unfortunately, there are hundreds, even thousands, of shady lenders out there who have made people question the integrity and lending practices of all mortgage lenders everywhere.

My objective is to E.M.P.O.W.E.R. people to make wise choices when choosing a lender and loan program and to give them a sense of confidence to make wise decisions concerning the financing of their home mortgage. Motivational speaker Les Brown said, "Don't let the negativity given to you by the world disempower you. Instead give to yourself that which empowers you." I believe what empowers a person is education. It's knowledge.

My goal is not to make you into a loan agent. My objective here is to provide you with some vital information, some secrets about the mortgage industry, that could save you thousands of dollars in closing costs, as well as tens of thousands of dollars over the life of your loan.

In the next few chapters you will find yourself being *motivated* and *empowered*. A definition of empowerment is: *to equip or supply with an ability; to give somebody power or authority; to authorize or enable*. Imagine, after reading this book, being equipped with the tools needed and possessing a new confidence to work with any lender. No matter what is placed in front of you, you will be confident you have the authority to ask and request the key documents which reveal the "true cost" of what is being proposed to you. This, in turn, will safeguard you and your family from falling victim to any predatory lending.

Take control and get empowered!

Equipping

Equipping yourself is one of the best things you can do to achieve empowerment. It doesn't matter what the task at hand may be. If you are better equipped, then the odds for success are exponentially greater. My senior year in high school I played football. I wasn't a terribly big kid; however, speed was my friend and my ally. The last game of the season was the "BELL" game. We played the local rival team Apple Valley High School for this Liberty Bell. Whichever team won the game got bragging rights for the rest of the year, and they took the bell to their school for the whole year and painted it their school colors. We had the bell for two years and wanted it for a third. It didn't look good for us at Victor Valley High School as our football team had only won a single game all season. Apple Valley had won the majority of their games and were play-off bound.

I remembered what my coach told the team the week before the game. He began to explain how we needed to better equip ourselves more than ever if we wanted to win.

We were going to watch more game footage, learn the players' strengths and weaknesses, focus on what we do best, and give a 110 percent in practice. We were to eat, sleep, and breathe what was up against us in the next five days, and if our heart was in it and our focus was clear, our team record would be irrelevant when we stepped out on the field. Needless to say, our team was focused and better equipped and we WON, 17–10!

You may have a good record, a poor record, or no record at all when it comes to dealing with a mortgage lender. As you read on, you will be equipping yourself with the secrets of the mortgage industry. *You will learn valuable trade secrets that will protect you from predatory lending.* You'll learn about the mortgage process. You'll understand what questions are critical to ask, and most important, I'll tell you about *documents you'll want to request* to make sure nothing is being hidden from you. You should never feel you are in competition with your lender. You are both supposed to be on the same side: YOUR side. By making this time investment, you will be equipping yourself to ensure the best mortgage at the fairest price for you and your family, and it will be a WIN-WIN situation for both you and your lender.

Mother Tongue

Our mother tongue is our first, or native, language. If you have gone through the lending process before, it may seem to you as if mortgage lenders speak a language all their own. They use terms that are foreign to us without taking the time to explain what it all means. Some of us become so overwhelmed by it that we find ourselves nodding along as they speak even when we don't understand everything they are saying. The mortgage industry is term-sensitive. You may have heard different terminology used when referring to the individual who works one on one with the client, such as: Loan Officer, Lender, Broker, Mortgage Broker, Banker, Mortgage Banker, Account Executive, etc. I will be referring to such individuals as "Loan Agents."

Tricky or unfamiliar terminology can be easily used to "sneak a fee" past you. I'm going to teach you to speak to mortgage lenders in *their* "mother tongue." It's not hard. I'm going to teach you some basic terms and coach you through the conversations you should have with your specific loan agent.

You may think you already know how to ask the questions you need answers to. Unfortunately, the predatory loan agent will take advantage of their client's ignorance and use their lack of understanding against them. Learning the mortgage language is understanding how to ask the *right* questions the *right* way at the *right* time.

A friend of mine was refinancing his home and asked me what my company charged in closing costs. I told him we charged a one percent origination fee and a processing fee. When he received his Good Faith Estimate, he noticed all the other fees that go into closing a loan. He called me perplexed and asked, "I thought you said my closing costs were only one percent plus a processing fee?" I felt terrible, and explained he did not ask me what the *total* closing costs were; he asked what *my company* charged. I assumed (*never assume by the way*) he knew there were other fees associated to the loan than those generated by my company. He hadn't asked the *right question* the *right way* at the *right time*. He understood what had happened, and I learned an important lesson about how to clearly communicate with a client and when to ask clarifying questions.

There are predatory loan agents who will prey on their clients' ignorance or lack of experience to secure their business, "sandbagging" them late into the process with fees they (the agents) knew about in the beginning. We will work together to make sure that doesn't happen to you.

Players

Do you know who all the "players" are involved in the loan process? You should. Each one of them affects the timing and quality of your loan, and you are paying each of them for their services. What are their roles? Why and when do they do what they do? Who establishes costs and whether or not they are fair? Are some fees negotiable? Are all the charges necessary? I have always tried to explain to my clients that I am not the only one who works on their loan. There are a variety of players in multiple offices working for different companies who work together to fund a loan. An important part of being empowered is understanding who's involved in the process. If you understand who's involved and what their roles are, you will have a better feel for the process you are going through (and paying for) and know whom to go to get the answers you need.

Open-eyes

As an empowered purchaser, you enter the process with "eyes wide open" as you go about finding an agent. Choosing teams is something we've all done since we were kids out on the playground. Remember when it was your turn to pick the team at recess, and everyone was shouting at you who your next pick should be? You had the pressure of wanting to pick a winning team and a cacophony of voices trying to convince you they were the best pick. Talk about pressure. Some things never change. Now we have loan agents clamoring to be on our team, trying to convince us that they can make us a winner. The stakes are higher now however, measured in tens or even hundreds of thousands of dollars rather than playground bragging rights.

When you choose a doctor or dentist, you are careful to make sure you choose someone whose skills and judgment you can trust, someone you can work well with, and one who is well regarded in the field. Choosing a company to handle your loan should be no different. I will show you what to look for in a lender and provide you with key interview questions for your initial conversations.

Watchful

Once you've chosen a team and begun the loan process, do you know what to watch for to make sure your loan is on time and on target? Did you know that there are government protocols that both the loan agent and the lending institution must adhere to? Did you know that there are laws requiring particular disclosures be given to you at the very beginning? Did you know if your agent couldn't produce a lock confirmation sheet, that the bank may not have actually "locked in" your rate? Of course you don't, but you can bet your loan agent does. Learning what to watch for will help make sure you get what you paid to receive. You will know when an unexpected fee "materializes" on your loan documents and if your agent is trying to pad his or her paycheck by using codes rather than dollar amounts. We'll walk through this together so you are confident in your ability to read and understand your loan documents.

Exposure

Do you remember what it feels like to wake up at night for the first time in a new bedroom and stumble toward the door? You're not sure where the light switch is and you keep waiting to bang your shin on a piece of furniture as you make your way forward. Negotiating the loan process can feel the same way. In this section we'll "flip the switch" and bring the relationship between the loan agent and the lending institution into the light! Did you know when loan agents quote you an interest rate, they are in most cases quoting their paycheck? It's true! Why do you think it's in their interest to sell you a higher rate? Generally speaking, the higher the rate the bigger the paycheck.

There is one word that is universal to all loan agents, no matter if they work for a Mortgager Broker or your local bank. That word determines their pay and/or bonus and it's *Rebate* – the great equalizer. I'll expose how rebate relates to your loan and how it affects the relationship between your lender and your loan agent. Your new-found understanding will give you the leverage you need to keep things fair and balanced when it comes to the fees and interest rates you pay.

Revelation

Revealing how a magic trick is done removes the mystery and intrigue behind it, and something that once seemed "mystical" becomes commonplace. When I was in the fourth grade I learned a trick out on the playground. You take a deck of cards and divide them in half. You put all the black cards with the black cards and all the red cards with the red cards. You ask the other person, as you are holding the now two decks face down in your hands, to pick a deck. The deck they pick, you ask them to pick a card out of it, any card. They pick the card and show their friends. You then take the other deck they did not originally choose and ask them to insert it anywhere they would like into the deck. You would proceed to shuffle the deck face down. Then, you, and only you, look at the face of the cards and quickly identify their card – it's the only one of its color in the deck. You show them their card and amaze them with your skill.

One day I was performing my trick and the schoolyard bully piped up and revealed how I was doing the trick. All the other kids laughed and walked away, no longer impressed with my magic because they could now do it themselves, and I had to find a new career.

Revealing a magician's trick takes the drama out of

what is happening before you. When you are dealing with hundreds of thousands of dollars, you want to remove as much drama from the process as you can. *UnMasking the Mortgage Madness* is going to reveal to you the tricks of the mortgage trade and save you from unnecessary drama.

This book will educate and E.M.P.O.W.E.R. you in the decisions you make. It is exciting for me to hear the testimonies of people who have applied the practices outlined in this book and have saved themselves thousands of dollars in their closing costs and over the life of their loan because they were able to unmask the madness.

Over the years I have had the pleasure of doing business with a lot of great clients. Everyone unique, but yet all of them having the same goal: to live an empowered life.

I hope you find this book humorous, enlightening, and most important, empowering!

To you and your future!

Rick Bulman
Your Trusted Mortgage Consultant
Mortgage Wise, LLC

Chapter

1

What You Want in a Lender

Abraham Lincoln, *"Character is like a tree and reputation like it's shadow. The shadow is what we think of it; the tree is the real thing."* Go with a bank or mortgage company that is the real thing.

remember my eleventh wedding anniversary. I surprised my wife with a weekend get-away – just the two of us. I had the whole event planned. I booked a room at a very nice hotel in Victoria, B.C., and our means of transportation was by seaplane from Seattle to Victoria.

We checked our luggage at a quaint commuter airport and waited for our flight. When we walked out to the dock to board the plan, we were warmly greeted by the pilot who looked to be a fit man of 60 years or so. He began to detail the flight plan and prepared us for what we could expect on a small craft flight. It was obvious to us that he was very experienced and his manner was extremely reassuring. When he finished his announcements, he invited us to board the plane. The boarding process on a small, floating plane can be difficult and the pilot was prepared to help. He offered his hand to my wife, assisting her and every other woman boarding the airplane. He was an impressive gentleman with a very professional demeanor. During our flight we did indeed experience some turbulence, but we were never worried. The pilot had spent some time preparing us, so the turbulence didn't make us too nervous.

On the way back, however, there was a completely different story. Prior to boarding, we were not greeted or acknowledged by anyone. In the place of the friendly, professional pilot there was a young 20-something gentleman, hands in pockets, looking disinterested and rather unapproachable. The passengers weren't sure if they should board the plane or not. The young man did little to replicate the pleasant experience of the first pilot. In fact, his lack of communication was quite disturbing. My wife was the first to board. She stood there looking at the young pilot, thinking he would help her into the plane. But instead of assisting like our first pilot, this young man managed only a stiff wave meant to communicate, "Get in already. People are waiting."

On the flight back we encountered heavy head winds, which shook the small plane. The turbulence continued, and I began to get uncomfortable. I started to sweat, and my stomach was in knots. It was difficult to understand why I was really nervous at first. We had turbulence on the first flight, and I was not worried at all. Soon I realized it was my discomfort with the pilot. I simply did not have confidence in the man flying the plane. He did nothing to inspire trust. His lack of professionalism made me feel that he was as poor a pilot as he was a communicator, which was amplified by the contrast between this pilot and our first one. Our first pilot was great! He put us at ease. We felt as though he had total command of his profession and that we were in good hands. This young pilot was the polar opposite.

While dealing with a mortgage company may not carry the same life-threatening possibilities, I often think of this story when I am explaining to people what they should look for in a lender.

It doesn't matter what bank or mortgage company you choose, you will undoubtedly experience a little turbulence in the loan process. Sometimes the turbulence will feel minor, or sometimes it will feel like you've hit a 50-foot air pocket. Your comfort level throughout the loan process will be directly related to your degree of confidence in your loan agent. Will this loan agent be more like the first pilot or the second one? How will he or she handle the times of turbulence? Do you feel this agent has the ability to bring everything back to a smooth cruising altitude?

How might you find that great loan agent that inspires confidence, one that has command of his business? What are some ground rules that people need to pay attention to when choosing a bank, mortgage company, and/or loan agent for their home financing needs? I'm going to identify six ground rules you can use to help you pick a finance company and loan agent.

GR #1: A stable and reputable company.

Find a company that is stable and has been around for a while. By doing so, you decrease the risk of working with a company that is potentially undercapitalized. If possible, work with a company and loan agent that is local to your area. Working with a bank or loan agent who is in another time zone can be, at times, a frustrating experience. Imagine that you encounter a serious problem with your loan and cannot get in touch with your loan agent. It would be so much easier to simply walk into a local office and sort things out. I was talking with a lady who was trying to refinance her home and her closing costs had changed and her rate had gone up. Her out-of-state loan agent was not returning her calls in a timely fashion. She felt frustrated and incapacitated. It is a helpless feeling.

You also want to choose a company that has a good reputation. You need to ask, why should I work with you and your company? What proof do they have that they operate sufficiently, responsibly, and ethically? Are they known for quality of products and service? You want a company whose reputation precedes it, one who is genuine in its quest to better benefit you and not just their bottom line. I like this quote from Abraham Lincoln, *"Character is like a tree and reputation like its shadow. The shadow is what we think of it; the tree is the real thing."* Go with a bank or mortgage company that is the real thing.

GR #2: A seasoned loan agent.

What makes someone a seasoned loan agent? You may think it's time on the job. I would beg to differ. Tenure is not necessarily the best measurement in finding a quality loan agent. The number of transactions the loan agent has completed is a much stronger barometer of a seasoned agent. Think about it. If you ask your loan agent, "How long have you been in the business?" and the agent says, "four years" it sounds like a substantial amount of time, right? But the one thing the loan agent may not have explained is that those four years have been with seven different mortgage companies and he had been discharged or forced to leave due to low productivity. Many of the poor loan agents write fewer than six mortgages per year. Let me ask you, how much experience do you think one would get doing six mortgage transactions a year? Not very much!

It is unfortunate, but a lot of loan agents go from company to company because they simply cannot meet their company's monthly minimum quota of production. Therefore, they find themselves jumping to the next mortgage company.

There is a huge difference in being *in* the mortgage world and doing *well* in the mortgage world. When I was the Vice President of Sales for Driscoll Financial Services, I would interview a lot of potential candidates and most of them claimed to be seasoned loan agents. When asked very basic questions about the mortgage industry/process, they could not answer them. I don't care if their resume said seven years in the industry; I know people who were properly trained with just over a year or two experience who knew more about the industry simply because of the number of monthly transactions they completed. The experiences learned over multiple transactions were what grew them to be the professional they are today. You will feel more confident knowing your loan agent has successfully executed up to 40 plus transactions (and that's actually a conservative number) a year for the last four years.

When my third son Jared was born, we did not have our regular doctor. Our family doctor of many years had delivered our other two boys as well as over 3000 other babies in his career. He had delivered twins and even a few sets of triplets. We were more than confident that if anything went wrong, our doctor had already experienced the situation and would know what to do. Now, we were living in California when Jared was born and due to the type of health insurance we had, we would not know who was going to actually deliver our child until the birth took place. When the time came, a young lady walked into the hospital room looking more like she should have been waving pom-poms at the college football game than delivering babies and announced, "I'm your doctor." I thought to myself, "She's so young. Can she actually do this?" Her name badge did say "Doctor" so I surmised things would turn out well.

It wasn't too long before I realized things were not turning out well. My wife was having a difficult time pushing Jared out. I remembered her looking at me with fear in her eyes. She was exhausted and did not have the strength to push anymore, and I began to get very concerned. She commented that she was not feeling normal compared to the other two births, and she was getting scared. I finally had asked the question that was pressing me for awhile, "By the way, how many babies have you delivered?" She said very proudly, "Almost a hundred." My initial thought was that seemed to be a fair amount of delivery experiences. Then I began to calculate if she'd delivered one baby every day or a few babies per week, that is less than six months experience! I almost died. A hundred may sound impressive when you find a carpenter who had built a hundred houses, but when it comes to babies, I want to hear that my doctor has delivered "thousands" not "a hundred." This doctor was doing little to ease the nervousness in the pit of my stomach. Fortunately, Jared finally came out, and both he and Tiffany left the hospital completely healthy.

Just as one would want a doctor who has a lot (thousands) of baby deliveries to secure a safe birthing experience, you want a loan agent who has done a lot of loan transactions. An experienced agent will minimize many of the potential setbacks one could face during the loan process. You need to understand there are hundreds of potential problems that pop up in a loan transaction, and the only way to learn, grow, and become skilled enough to handle and overcome such situations is through repetition.

Imagine something going sideways with your loan, and your loan agent says, "You are my eighth customer. Let me fix your problem." That may not necessarily trigger a wave of enthusiasm from you. If that less-experienced loan agent does not have a strong support system within the company, you may find yourself frustrated and a little intimidated. You'll find when working with an experienced professional, when a problem occurs, professionals will know exactly what to do.

GR #3: A versatile company.

You want to work with a mortgage company or bank that has a wide portfolio of loan products. Loan agents who work for such companies will offer more than a few loan programs or one or two financing options. I view it as the ability to speak more than one language. There are different worlds in the universe of mortgage banking. They are independent of one another, functioning differently from one another, and having their own set of rules and guidelines. However, they all have the same purpose of providing you with home financing. Let's acknowledge these different worlds briefly.

The 4 Basic Worlds Within the Mortgage Universe:

- The "A" paper world – This is where one qualifies for the best rates and best loan programs. Typically, they are considered "conforming cliental." Their personal scenario and/or loan scenario conform to the Fannie Mae or Freddie Mac loan program guidelines for strong borrowers.

- The "ALT – A" paper world – This is where someone or the loan scenario is not quite considered "A" paper, yet the client's portfolio is not necessarily bad enough to be considered a high-risk. These interest rates in this world can still be somewhat competitive.

- The "Sub-Prime" world – This is a client with a poor credit history or a weak overall portfolio. There are potentially many challenges and hurdles that a loan agent may need to conquer before submitting the loan for approval. "Sub-Prime" is more for the high-risk clients. However, there are many good programs that can get people into a home and place them on a path that will set them up for a better loan program in the future.

- The "Hard Money" lender world – This type of loan is really for people with credit scores below 500. For more understanding about credit scores, refer to the glossary of mortgage terms. Some banks will lend to clients with scores as low as 500. However, once one credit score drops below the 500 threshold, a bank may not finance them. That is where a "Hard Money" lender comes in. Note: The Hard Money lender will usually make the client have at least 35 to 45% in equity and will usually issue an interest-only payment at a high interest rate.

Let's get back to the idea about the ability to speak more than one language. Say you wanted to be a world traveler and see all the great sites our planet offers. You decide to use me as your guide. I would only be able to take you to English-speaking countries. We would not see all of Europe. I could not take you into the Asian countries. I couldn't even take you into Mexico. Why? I only speak English. In this sense, as your guide I would really be of little benefit to you. Take someone who is bilingual or who can speak four or five languages. If you use that person as your guide, your experience in traveling the world has now been broadened.

Choosing a lender is similar to choosing your travel guide. Some people may choose an "A" paper lender, not realizing they are not an "A" paper client. Maybe they have great credit but no money for a down payment, or they simply do not realize how poor their credit is. They choose an "A" paper lender, but their loan is denied. The client walks away feeling defeated with no sense of direction from the lender. Why? Because that lender only speaks "A" paper and is only familiar with "A" paper underwriting guidelines. The loan agent is unaware of the alternative lending options the "ALT –A" or "Sub-Prime" world offers. Simply put, they are not bilingual in the mortgage world.

When I am dealing with clients I will quickly identify what world or category they may be in. If they are "A" paper, then I put my "A" paper hat on. If the clients have poor credit and they are a "Sub-Prime" candidate, then I put a completely different hat on, because different rules apply. The four different mortgage worlds speak a different language and operate differently from each other. A good mortgage company/professional can wear more than one hat and speak more than one language concerning mortgage financing.

GR #4: **An honest loan agent.**

Honesty is huge and a must-have when it comes to choosing the right loan agent. Kin Hubbard, an American cartoonist, humorist, and journalist speaks to honesty in this way: "Honesty pays, but it doesn't seem to pay enough to suit some people." Unfortunately, his statement rings true, especially in the mortgage world. This whole book is geared toward helping people and revealing how predatory lending is running rampant through the lending industry. Remember, loan agents will qualify you to be their client, but equally you have the right to qualify them to see if they have what it takes to earn your business. Here are some initial things to be mindful of when interviewing/searching for an honest loan agent.

1) A professional – Listen for their language. You do not want someone who comes across shoddy, with winks, nods, and elbows to the side, as if to give you a special deal. They need to be courteous, respectful, and patient with you.

2) A good listener – Do you ever have a conversation with people and you feel like they are not even listening to you? You feel they are just waiting for you to stop speaking so they can talk. The honest loan agent will not push their agenda, but first listen to yours. Your conversation with them should never feel rushed. You

should feel their agenda is whatever your agenda is.

3) An accommodator – Honest lenders will always make you feel like they have your best interest in mind. They want to make your loan process as smooth as possible and will accommodate you in any way they can.

4) A CLEAR communicator – You never want to walk away confused. Honest loan agents will speak clearly and be forthright with you. If you have a question, they will give you the complete answer. You should never walk away wondering if they even answered your questions.

As you continue to read through this book, I will reveal in greater detail the tell-tell signs one needs to look out for in finding that honest loan agent.

GR #5: An available loan agent.

Being available is key to the client. To me there is nothing more frustrating than working with people and knowing I can only talk with them between a certain period of time in the day, like from 9:00 a.m. to 5:00 p.m. If I am working with a loan agent and I have what seems to be a BIG question, then I would like the ability to call my loan agent at 2:00 p.m. on a Saturday or 7:30 p.m. on a Thursday.

I am reminded of sitting down with some clients in their home on a Thursday evening. They had a lot of questions for me. Before I left, the wife asked why they should go with me rather than their bank. I simply reminded them that they would be hard pressed to get the loan agent in their bank to come to their home late on a Thursday evening. I encouraged her to ask her bank whom she could call if she had a random question late on a Saturday or even on a Sunday. She replied, "Point well made."

You want loan agents who will be available to you when you need them. It can be very uncomfortable and even nerve racking, feeling that something is wrong with your transaction and having to wait until nine in the morning on a Monday to get your question answered. If you are trying to borrow a large sum of money, then I believe you have the right to have your questions answered in a timely fashion.

GR #6: A great communicator.

Good loan agents will communicate through the process. You should never find yourself guessing what is going to happen next in the loan process. It is their job to convey the order of steps to you and the timeline in which it will take to fund your loan. In the beginning you want to set a foundation for good, clear communication. Your loan agents *should* ask how you prefer to communicate, home phone, work phone, cell phone, or email. If for some reason they do not, here are some basic questions to establish lines of communication:

- What are your hours of availability?

- What days of the week are you NOT available?

- What is your best means of communication? Email, cell phone, office phone, etc.

- Do you respond to text messaging? (*It's pretty popular today.*)

- If I try to contact you, how long will it take for you to typically get back to me before I should try again?

The last point is very important for your peace of mind. If your loan agent communicates he or she returns calls within an hour and three or more hours have passed, you have the right to call back. Do not feel like you are being an annoyance. A lot of clients feel their questions are too small, too basic, or too silly. Remember, your questions are never too small, basic, or silly to ask. You do not mortgage your home every month and therefore the expectation for you to know everything is simply not there. If your question is a big deal to you, then it's a big deal, period!

Picking the right lender/loan agent is key when getting a mortgage. Make sure whomever you choose to do business with, is with a stable and reputable company. Identify your loan agent as a *true* seasoned professional. Be sure the company is versatile in their loan products. Make sure your loan agent is available for you and your lines of communication are drawn early on in the process. Following the steps I outlined in this chapter can make the difference between a pleasant experience and a living nightmare, which costs you more money than you care to lose.

Chapter

2

What You <u>Don't</u> Want in a Lender

U.S. Clergyman Harry Emerson Fosdick said,
"He who chooses the beginning of a road chooses the
place it leads to. It is the means that determine the end."
The choice of lender in the beginning of your journey is
the means that will determine your end experience.

Remember in grade school being out on the playground getting ready to pick teams for a game everyone wanted to play? Everyone lined up along the fence. The two chosen captains strategically selected their players who would best position them for a win.

If you were a captain, you did not randomly pick kids to be on your team. You did not take the eenie, meenie, miney, moe approach. You selected your team very carefully. You analyzed the strengths and weaknesses of each player before coming to a decision, hopefully a decision that would bring you victory.

Choosing a company to get a home loan is a lot like picking a team out on the playground. The same strategies are in play in your thought process. If as a child we would pause and think through our decisions in choosing a team for a silly kid's game, how much more caution should we use in selecting a company that will lend us up to hundreds of thousands of dollars for a home?

Regardless if you were ever one of those captains out on the playground, you need to realize you are the captain now. You are the one who will choose who will be on your team. The scary part in all of this is when you were on the playground, you were picking from a group of kids you knew, probably your friends. However, choosing a lender is the equivalent of lining a group of kids along the fence you know absolutely nothing about. It makes choosing a winning team a little more difficult. This chapter will provide you with insight, which will better safeguard you from deciding on a lender you do not want.

U.S. Clergyman Harry Emerson Fosdick said, "He who chooses the beginning of a road chooses the place it leads to. It is the means that determine the end." You are getting ready to walk down the road to acquire a new mortgage. The choice of lender in the beginning of your journey is the means that will determine your end experience.

Here are five precautionary principles to protect you from choosing the wrong lender.

Principle #1: **Working with an unknown company.**

You want to do your due diligence in researching a company. It involves finding out as much information as you can to determine if it is a good fit for you and your family's needs.

Now, there are two major factors to be considered when selecting a lender. One, you want to make sure whomever you choose is not new to your area. Ideally you want someone who is local and familiar with the market. Two, you want to work with a mortgage company that has been in business for a good length of time. Working with a lender that has been through various trends in the market speaks to their stability and validity as a company, which are qualities you're looking for.

Here are some additional helpful hints in educating yourself about your lender of choice:

- Search their website (most mortgage lending institutions have a website).

- Read the executive profiles. You want experienced leadership behind your loan agent.

- Read testimonials from past clients.

- Read any materials published in the media, including newspapers, trade publications, and the Internet.

Principal #2: *Working with a lender that has too-good-to-be-true claims.*

I remember when I first learned about something seeming too good to be true. I was about 15 years of age. I went to get the mail one day and noticed an envelope addressed to my parents. It looked very official. It had a gold seal on the front and it read, "Congratulations, you're a finalist." I opened it to see what my parents were going to be potentially winning. There it was! My dreams had seemed to come true. We were going to be RICH! This letter stated my mom and dad were one of five finalists in the Publisher's Clearing House, and we were guaranteed $1 million dollars as a finalist and $10 million dollars if we won. All we had to do was mail in some codes.

After catching my breath I ran to my parents' room and banged on the door. My mom recalls me groaning and not speaking due to my excitement. When she realized what was going on she started to laugh. She began to explain that everyone receives an envelope such as this and everyone is a finalist. My heart sank as I heard these dreaded words for the first time, "Ricky, if it seems too good to be true, then more than likely it is."

If you are human, at one point in your life you have probably fallen for the too-good-to-be-true ad. Remember seeing ads such as these?

Make $4000 A MONTH Working from Home!!! Call now for more information.

LOSE 10 lbs A WEEK - and EAT ANYTHING YOU WANT!! Easy, painless, safe weight-loss formula, GUARANTEED to work!

Find the college scholarships and GRANTS NO ONE ELSE KNOWS ABOUT. Each year $$$$ of financial aid goes unclaimed because no one knew to ask for it. Send just $5.00 for our guide that could SAVE you THOUSANDS!

More than likely, you've seen these ads before. They claim to have the secret to make one rich, beautiful, and happy.

The same planning and strategies are in place when advertising for a mortgage company. Many people fall for the same pitch/ad every day from lenders. The number one goal is to get you to call. They will get very creative with their marketing and do whatever it takes to get you to do so. The sad thing is, manipulation plays a big part in it.

Be mindful of the too-good-to-be-true ad, companies who claim to have the lowest rates around, and the lowest closing costs, or they are the ONLY establishment that offers a specific loan program.

I am reminded of a young couple who walked into a development under construction. The builder's in-house lender greeted them. The loan agent said, "We have a special going right now. If you use me, I can give you last year's interest rates." The couple believed him! It was a sales gimmick. You can't give away last year's interest rates. If that were true, then why stop at last year's rates? Why not go back a few years and give the lowest rate I have ever seen: 4.750% on a 30-year fixed.

People want to hear what they want to hear, and they want to believe the unbelievable. Lenders know this and use it to their advantage, especially, the Predatory Loan Agent (*PLA*). If you come across something that seems too good to be true, remember it probably is.

Principal #3: *Working with a company that keeps banker's hours.*

Banker's hours, by definition, means a short working day. You need to ask yourself, what is your preference? Would you like your loan agent's availability to *only* be between 9:00 a.m. to 5:00 p.m., or would you prefer to work with someone you can reach beyond normal working hours? I would think the latter.

I remember being at a birthday party, and my cell phone began to ring. It was about 10:30 p.m. It happened to be a client of mine, the McKinseys. I still recall the quick stare from my wife. I could read her mind, "Do not answer it!" Going against the stare, I answered my phone. The conversation lasted not more than two minutes. I then felt an explanation was in order, as I did not want to be in the doghouse. I went on to let her know the McKinseys rarely call and the fact that they were calling at an unusual time warranted my attention.

They had received some paperwork in the mail from the bank. They were confused and very much alarmed by what they had read. They needed an explanation. I told them the figures were not from me and to disregard them. I assured them their loan program, interest rates, and closing costs had not changed. I remembered what they said to me before they hung up: "We're sorry for calling so late. We started to feel we could not afford the financing of the home we were purchasing based on the numbers that were on these forms. It was eating us up, and we could not wait to talk with you."

A two-minute conversation allowed the McKinseys to go to bed that night without the fear of losing their dream home. From a loan agent's perspective, there was no need to worry, but from the clients' perspective, there was every reason to worry. My availability meant the world to my clients. My question to you is, when working with a loan agent how important is the agent's availability?

Principal #4: *Working with a company that only specializes in minimal loan products.*

My kids love to save their money and go to the store to buy a toy. A lot of times they do not necessarily know what it is they want to buy. There is one store we always go to first, which offers a lot of variety, Toys "R" Us. They have anything from stuffed animals, to video games, to action figures, to bikes, and skateboards. Nine times out of ten, they always can find what they are looking for.

Discovering the right loan product is often like that experience. You know you want/need a loan, but the magic question is what kind of loan? When dealing with a lender who is well versed in many loan programs, you are presented with many options. Usually one option will harmonize more with your future goals, and that is the one you select. When choosing, a lender's versatility is important!

Watch out for companies that are considered cookie cutter companies. Their specialty in loan programs is very limited. In words from the previous chapter, they only speak one language. Working with such a company limits your potential in finding just the right loan for you.

You want to work with a lender who offers options. Here are some quick questions you can ask the prospective lender:

- Are you primarily an "A" paper bank/broker? (*Hopefully they say no.*)

- Are you able to finance in the "A" paper world, Alt-A world, and Sub-Prime world? (*The best answer to this question is YES!*)

- What programs do you specialize in? (*You want to hear them say, "I do not just specialize in one program, but I am well-versed in many loan programs.*)

- If going through a bank, how many investors does your

company work with? (*The investor is the one who will purchase the loan from the bank once the loan has closed. The more investors a bank has, the more negotiations your banker will have with different companies to find you the best loan. He or she can shop investors*).

- If going through a mortgage broker, how many wholesale lenders do you work with? (*The mortgage broker/loan agent acts as a mediator between the wholesale lender and the client. The wholesale lenders do not work directly with the public. They simply provide loans through mortgage brokers to the clients that come through their door. The more wholesale lenders a mortgage broker has, the more negotiations they will have to find you the best loan. They can shop wholesale lenders*).

If the prospective loan agent's answers are favorable to these suggestions, then you are dealing with a lender who allows you to be in control. You as a client gain control when you have the ability to choose what is best for you. The greatest power given is the power of choice. Work with a lender who does not rob you of that power. Take control and choose your loan program.

Principal #5: *Working with a Rookie Loan Agent (RLA)*

If you choose to work with someone who is new in the industry, you need to be very careful. Over the years, I have witnessed some horrific mistakes made by loan agents who would be considered "rookies" due to their lack of experience.

There is one common mistake made by the RLA. They

all seem to think back on their past sales experiences and believe the same sales techniques, experiences, and successes will transfer over into the world of selling mortgages. It is one of the biggest hurdles the RLA will need to over come.

There is a different mentality that people seem to have when sorting out financing on a home verses a car, furniture, cell phone, etc. It's a bigger purchase that carries more liability. Therefore, people tend to be a lot more cautious. The same games they played in selling cars, cell phones, furniture, clothing, bottled water, etc., to past cliental do not carry over well in the mortgage arena.

Rookie mistakes have been known to cost people tens of thousands of dollars. I know of one case where a client had sold his home, but the financing on the new home fell through. The RLA simply didn't know what he was doing. The only thing he did do well was talk a good game.

Here are some of the pitfalls the "rookie loan agent" will fall into:

- *Rookies are very zealous*

RLAs will often be "yes" people. They say yes to anything and everything. Why? To get your business. They work out of fear. Fear of losing you as a client. They are simply scared to be honest. They are too afraid to say no. How often do you come across something in life that is yes, yes, yes? When a salesman tells me no, it actually reassures me he is being honest with me. Ask yourself this question: If you *truly* cannot get the mortgage financing you want, would you want someone who tells you yes and leads you to believe in a false reality or someone who will tell you no? Ultimately, I think we all are comforted by the occasional no.

▪ *Rookies lack product knowledge*

There are literally thousands of loan programs to choose from. There are programs with special characteristics coupled with specific underwriting guidelines. If overlooked, an inexperienced loan agent can cost a client time and money. RLAs are often unfamiliar with the fine details of the many programs.

Here are a few:

- A couple asks if they can do 100% financing. The RLA says only if they have a 580 credit score. The RLA verifies the score is 580, and lets them know they qualify. After a $450 appraisal and two weeks of the clients' time, however, the loan is denied. Why? The RLA did not realize that with a 580 credit score, the client must not have any "mortgage lates." These clients had two mortgage lates in the last 12 months. A very rookie mistake.

- A client inquires about a "Stated Income" loan. The client is self-employed and has great credit scores with 10% for a down payment. The RLA very well may say the deal can be done. However, when the file gets to underwriting, it is rejected. The client has been self-employed for less than a year. When it comes to stated income for a self-employed individual, banks require two years of ownership. Nothing less.

- People just bought a house, and within the first six months want to maximize the new equity they've incurred to pull some cash out and refinance. The RLA lets them know it should not be a problem, but the RLA does not realize the client lacks what the bank refers to as seasoning. Most banks' (*but not necessarily all*) guidelines will not accept a new appraisal for value because the clients have less than six months or less than a year's time (season) in their home. The banks will only accept the original purchase price as value. This guideline has stopped many refinances from taking place. It was simply too soon for the clients.

I remember my first year in the mortgage industry. A client called me and asked me three specific questions. She asked, "Do you offer a 5-year adjustable rate mortgage?" I assured her we did. She asked, "Do you offer interest-only programs?" I let her know we did. Then she asked, "Do you offer 100% financing?" I let her know we could accommodate her in that way as well. She was happy to hear my answers and wanted to move forward. Her loan was denied.

My boss came to me and explained we do offer all three of those financing options, but not at the same time (the loan at that time did not exist; however, it does today in some non-conforming markets). I told him I didn't understand why because the client had "A" paper credit. My boss showed me the guidelines for "A" paper and that you cannot do a 100% financing. The guidelines limit the client to a 95% financing. It was a classic rookie mistake. Fortunately, my boss presented an alternative to the client and she was still happy. That was a mistake I vowed to never make again.

▪ *Rookies cannot see the future*

Many times a RLA focuses on the now. The experienced loan agent has the ability to foresee any potential pitfalls in the loan process. Only experience can give you such ability. It's seeing scenarios over and over again that begins to formulate accurate predictions concerning the process.

I had a client who wanted to buy his friend's house. I knew the house would not appraise for more than $198,000. His friend, the seller, had a pre-payment penalty on his loan. I was concerned what the pay-off on his loan would be. The seller told me to go ahead and order the appraisal because he really wanted to sell his home to his friend. He went on to explain whatever the pay-off came in at he would eat the cost. A RLA would more than likely go through with the transaction. However, I told the seller I did not feel comfortable with ordering the appraisal, because I have seen pay-off statements come in a lot higher than what was anticipated. I explained since he had already ordered the pay-off statement, I would wait until I had a chance to review it before spending $400 of my client's money on the appraisal.

I was right. The pay-off came in A LOT higher than what the seller had thought. Therefore, the seller could not get the proceeds he was hoping for out of the sale, and the transaction died. My experience had safeguarded my client the expense of a $400 dollar appraisal. Sometimes having a true understanding of how loans work can save the client a lot of heartache, time, and money.

• *Rookies can give bad advice*

Rookies have a tendency to give wrong advice. They are not familiar with the ins and outs of the industry. They try to guide the client as best they can. Sometimes the direction they give ends up being poor counsel.

I have heard RLAs instruct their clients to not make their mortgage payment during the refinance process. If you are not an experienced loan agent and you do not close the loan in a timely fashion, you run the risk of the clients incurring a 30-day late mark on their credit report. Many times that has automatically disqualified the client from the original quoted rate and loan program. The client may need to take a different loan program with a higher interest rate due to a now derogatory mark against the mortgage.

There was a couple who owned a home in the central California. They were relocating to Seattle, Washington, and they wanted to refinance and borrow against the equity of their current home to purchase a second home. They were involved with a loan agent who would be considered a rookie. The couple was anxious to move to Seattle to begin the searching process. The RLA let them know it was okay for them to make the move now that the loan was approved. The clients informed the RLA that the spouse would need to quit her job and questioned if that was okay? The RLA assured them the underwriter had already underwritten the loan and it was fine. They made the move, found a home they loved, and put in an offer.

Just before their refinance in California was finished, the bank wanted to do a verification of employment. The RLA did not realize that might happen. At that time the bank found out the client's spouse had quit, which in turn, halted the process and the file was denied. They also lost the home they put an offer on because they now did not qualify because of their lack of income.

These people uprooted their lives and made decisions based on a pseudo professional. When working with a rookie loan agent, you run the risk of that same type of experience. It is unfortunate that such inexperienced loan agents make minor mistakes. However, it is those minor mistakes that carry major consequences for their clients.

You owe it to yourself to do your homework in choosing a lender. Remember the five precautionary principles. Choose to work with a company/loan agent that carries a good reputation. Work with a lender who shoots straight from the hip and does not have misleading advertising. Select a lender that you can access beyond normal business hours, and most importantly, choose to work with a seasoned loan agent. Do not allow lack of experience to cost you.

Chapter

3

Behind the Scenes Part 1

What a Predatory Loan Agent wants to hide

The steps of discovery will empower you to take control of one of the biggest financial investments of your life. This behind the scenes look will help you distinguish between mortgage myth and your reality.

Whenever my family and I rent a movie, we love to watch all the special features that are on the DVD. We love to watch the deleted scenes and the bloopers. The "behind the scenes" or the "making of the movie" are features I am entertained by. It's fascinating to watch how they create an object or scene through computer animation. A layman's way of putting it is through "trick photography." In many cases, you would not even question the veracity of what you are watching.

The Discovery Channel one day aired the making of *Bad Boys II*, with Martin Lawrence and Will Smith. In this episode, they revealed how they shot a high-pace, high-energy car scene. Martin Lawrence and Will Smith were in pursuit. In the midst of chasing someone at high speeds, there was an 18-wheeler pulling quite a few cars. The cars on the 18-wheeler began to fall off the back of the truck. Cars were crashing into one another and blowing up. All the while, Martin Lawrence and Will Smith were dodging the chaos as they stay in pursuit.

To my surprise artists drew a lot of that car chase scene. What I saw with the naked eye and thought to be real was indeed a computer-generated image. The artists were so good that they tricked the audience into thinking something was real when in fact it wasn't. They knew if the scene was packed with high-speed action and quick camera work, coupled with phenomenal artistic ability, the viewing audience would never realize a lot of the scene was actually computer generated.

Did you know the mortgage industry has a lot of "behind the scenes" action? You could label it as "trick photography" or "tricks of the trade." A clever, unethical loan agent (or PLA) can paint such a picture of promise, but the reality of what one is getting is quite different than what has been communicated.

I am going to share with you some of the predatory loan agents' behind-the-scenes activities, which unfortunately takes place within the mortgage industry. You will learn some of the tricks of the trade. Would you like to know what is going through a PLA's mind as they are listening to you? Are they steering the conversation without your knowing it? Are you playing a game of which you are not even aware? With your newfound awareness, you will be able to better safeguard yourself from such tactics.

The lending market today has an immense amount of new loan programs. Therefore, there are more people today who can qualify for home loans. However, due to the unscrupulous lenders' business transactions, they have taken advantage of the situation and placed borrowers in unnecessarily costly and inappropriate loans. By doing this they are serving their own financial gain. This is recognized as predatory lending.

Not all lenders operate unscrupulously. However, it does become a problem when predatory lending practices or "tricks" become part of the deal. Let's identify some of the "tricks of the trade" unethical lenders/loan agents seem to pull with their clients.

Behind the Scenes Trick #1: **The Bait and Switch!**

I know what it is like to be a victim of the bait and switch. My wife and I were in the market to by an SUV. We wanted one that would fit our family of six comfortably. I started to call around to the local dealers and found a dealer who promised me he could get us a new model for the payment we wanted. I asked him if he was sure. I told him I did not want to make the 20-minute drive to his establishment to find out things had changed. He placed me on hold as he went to confer with his manager. He assured me he could meet our needs. Again, I pressed him to see if he was sure. I reiterated that I did not want to haul my entire family to his car lot to have the transaction not take place. He promised me everything would be okay.

We made the trip to the car dealership. We asked for our salesman by name, and he came out to greet us. However, he said he was just called away to another lot to address an issue, but Michael (another salesman) had been brought up to speed and was aware of our needs and would be assisting us through the rest of the transaction.

Michael suddenly wanted to take us for a test drive. I told him we would after I receive confirmation that I could still get the SUV for the price I wanted. He had asked what I thought the payment would be. I informed him of my discussion with the other salesman. He explained there was no way I could get the vehicle for that amount. It would cost at least $150.00 more a month. I strongly urged him to go speak with his manager about my earlier conversation. He returned letting me know the manager had no such conversation with the previous salesman.

I had just then been a victim of the Bait and Switch. I was told one thing to get me into the door and the reality of my situation was much different than I thought. Luckily, I only wasted about an hour of my time. Unfortunately, people who are a victim of the Bait and Switch in the mortgage industry lose a lot more than just an hour of their time. Sometimes it is over a month, where an emotional and financial investment has been made.

This is a horrible tactic when it comes to selling mortgages to clients. A PLA will be positive and lead the clients to believe they are qualified for a particular product. It is common in predatory lending to make such claims when they have yet to run their clients' credit to assess their qualifications.

How can you fully trust your loan agent's quote if you have not given any personal information? How can loan agents properly qualify clients if they have yet to review their credit report? Watch that your loan agent doesn't become your "yes" man or woman just to get your business.

Once PLAs have tricked the clients into doing business with them, they begin the necessary research to see if indeed they can even offer what they quoted earlier. If the agents cannot qualify them, then they will begin to scramble and look for other options, all the while not advising the client of what is happening.

Predatory Loan Agents (PLAs) will utilize the Bait and

Switch sales tactic mostly within these four loan components:

- *Fees:* The PLA promises fewer fees in the beginning of the transaction. When it comes to signing the final paperwork, suddenly there are more fees.

- *Interest Rate:* The PLA will often quote an interest rate that is pleasing to the ear of the client. The client may not qualify for the quoted interest rate. The PLA very well may want to earn a bigger commission check, so the client's interest rate is increased to make more rebate. All the while the PLAs excuse the interest rate bump with persuasive language.

- *Loan Programs:* The PLA may sell the clients on the wonderful features of a loan program they do not qualify for. Once the clients commit to a false reality, the PLA delivers the sobering news. Again, flowery speech explains the loan program change away.

- *Pre-Payment Penalty:* The PLA often (*selectively*) forgets to inform the client of any pre-payment penalties the loan may have. The client discovers the penalty when signing the final paperwork. The PLA will explain the *un*realistic benefits of having such a penalty. Many times the client will begrudgingly sign the loan documents.

Often with the Bait and Switch (when it is time for signing the final paperwork) the results are much different than the earlier conversations. The PLA will begin to make excuses; nonetheless, the client is at the signing table and at the eleventh hour is put in an unfair position to decide whether or not to proceed. Nine times out of ten, the client will unhappily agree to sign. The PLA is happy because he just earned a commission on another deal. It happens all too often. In Chapter Seven, "Asking the Right Questions the Right Way," you will be given tools to better safeguard yourself from being a victim of the Bait and Switch.

Behind the Scenes Trick #2: *Interest Rate Quoting!*

When clients come to speak to a loan agent, they usually have two things on their mind; the closing costs and the interest rate. The client's first question a lot of times will be, "What is the lowest rate I can get?" It's really too vague a question. It is literally the same as if you asked, "What is the price for cars today?" How do you answer that question? "What do you want?" would be my reply. Do you want new or used? Do you want to purchase or lease? Do you want a sports car, sedan, or truck? Do you want American-made or imported? Again, it depends on what you want. It is too vague a question. There are too many unanswered questions for me to just say any number.

When it comes to mortgage loans the same rules apply. There are too many compensating factors for a loan agent to just ambiguously quote rates. When a client asks, "What is the lowest rate you can get me?" My response has always been, "What do you want?"

I begin to explain there are many compensating factors that come into play. Their credit score, their overall credit report, how long they plan on keeping the loan, the loan amount (large loan amounts, known as Jumbo Loans may have higher interest rates). What kind of home are they financing (manufactured, single family residence, multi-unit)? Equity is an issue. Do the clients have equity, or are they financing 100% of the property value? The list goes on. Good, honest lenders will not quote you an interest rate immediately because they know the truth of this fact. You want to work with lenders who will do their due diligence before quoting you any figures.

PLAs know that people are very rate sensitive, and they utilize the interest rate as a sales tactic to get your business. Quoting an interest rate has been considered a trick of the trade. The ability to convince people they can only qualify for a high interest rate is *unfortunately* a glorified unethical practice. Here are two common tricks in quoting interest rates:

Quoting the lowest rate possible

PLAs will quote the lowest rate possible while knowing the quoted rate will have to be bought down. The client is unaware of the actual cost to buy down the interest rate. The buy down cost could equal two or more points. Buying down the rate means the ability to permanently lower your interest rate through paying extra points. Points equal percentages. A half-a-point equals half a percent (.500%), one point equals one percent, two points equal two percent, etc. These are fees charged on the Good Faith Estimate to buy down the interest rate. For example, Mr. Smith is offered 6.500% on a 30-year fixed mortgage. For "one point" cost to him (in addition to his origination fee), he may be able to lower the interest rate to 6.000%. Note: one point cost does not always guarantee a full-half percent lower in the interest rate. The more points one pays, the lower the interest rate one can get. However, there is a limit to how much a client can buy down their rate. In other words, you cannot buy down your rate all the way to a one percent mortgage. It is NOT always a good idea to buy down the interest rate. It has been proven to be a case-by-case basis.

Quoting the lowest rate possible misleads clients into agreeing to work with them. It is a dishonest way of earning business. The loan agents falsely lead the clients into believing they can acquire this astronomically low rate, all the while not advising them of the high cost. Usually this type of loan agent will reveal the reality of these costs in the eleventh hour. At this point, the clients may feel they have no choice but to move forward. Quoting the lowest rate possible can be a gimmick.

Quoting an interest rate and then quoting a lower rate

Predatory loan agents are about taking advantage of their clients' lack of understanding. They know clients will not request certain documents to unveil the reality of the cost of the loan.

For example, a client may be offered a 6.5% interest rate on a loan program with a 1% origination fee. However, the PLA goes on to explain for a 1% discount point, the client can get a 6.125% interest rate. The clients believe they are buying down their rate. The problem with this scenario is the client technically can qualify for the lower rate without having to pay the extra point. However, they are unaware of this fact because of how the quote was offered. The PLA is fairly confident the clients are not aware of the proper documents to request, which reveal whether they really had to buy down their interest rate. The clients will have great difficulty finding the truth of the offer. Because of this reality, it makes getting away with selling a higher interest rate fairly easy. Interest rate quoting is something to be mindful of.

Behind the Scenes Trick #3: **Selling the "NO FEE" loan!**

There are things in life that are rare. One of them is getting something for nothing. Usually there is a cost when acquiring something of value. The other day I received something for free. I was at one of my favorite places on earth, Starbucks. When going through the drive thru, I found the line to be long and the wait to be longer. When I came up to the window, the lady handed me my coffee. She went on to explain how my coffee would be free due to the long wait. I graciously accepted this wonderful gift. As I drove off I began to imagine what it would be like if every company operated the same way. Imagine being in an electronics store waiting in a long line to purchase the 50-inch plasma television you've always wanted. When you reach the cashier, to your surprise, they say, "We're sorry for the long wait. This plasma television is on the house, our apologies." Better yet, you are shopping for your dream car, and you have to wait for the next available salesperson. Your wait tends to be longer than usual, and the manager comes to greet you and says, "We're sorry for the wait, your car will be on us today. Enjoy!"

I'm sure that sounds absurd. To even think any of that would be a reality would be ridiculous. The bewilderment I find is people actually believe they can get something for nothing, especially from a mortgage company. Clients literally believe they can obtain a free loan from a lender. However, the problem has not originated in the hearts of people to solicit such a ridiculous request. The problem has originated in the mortgage industry itself. Banks and mortgage brokers have falsely advertised "No Fee" loans as a ploy to get business. People love to view their Good Faith Estimate (*GFE*) and see no fees on there. Banks and mortgage companies know they can structure a loan in a specific way to communicate such a deal. The reality would be much different if they only knew the truth.

Let's get practical for a moment. I've always described the mortgage process as being made up of a team of people. Take a football team for example. There are many positions on a football team. All have different responsibilities, yet all work toward a common goal. To win! The same is true for all the companies (players) who work on a client's file. There are different companies or departments with different functions, but all work toward the common goal of funding the client's loan. These different companies and/or departments all need to get compensated for their services.

Although we will go in greater detail about the different entities that participate in the loan process (and their functions) in Chapter Ten, let's briefly identify some of the participants:

- **Brokers or Banks** — Originate and facilitate the loan

- **Underwriters** — Underwrite the loan

- **Processors** — Process the loan prior to underwriting

- **Appraiser** — Appraises the subject property, if needed

- **Escrow** — Facilitates a financial agreement between two parties as an equal third party member

- **Title** — Deals with property titles and issues title insurance

- **County** — Records the loan

- **Current lender** — (Selling a home or refinancing) Has pay-off fees and miscellaneous charges to close out the loan

- **Notary** — Notarizes documents

Each entity has a job to do. A job that requires compensation. What authority does your loan agent have to make up to 10 different people/companies do their job for free for a complete stranger? Does Bob from Bob's Mortgage Company have the authority to waive title and escrow fees? Even if he owned the title and escrow company, how long would he stay in business paying his employees but not charging for the services they provide? Not long.

I was doing a loan for a real estate agent. He said he wanted minimal fees and wanted a free appraisal. I informed him I did not own the appraisal company and therefore could not waive his appraisal costs. I went on to explain he would have to speak with the owner of the company to see if he would give him a free appraisal. The real estate agent was confused because he thought loan agents could waive such costs. I assured him the reality was we could not.

Here is the behind-the-scenes trick to making prospective clients believe they are getting a free deal. The loan agent typically makes a rebate on a client's loan. Rebate is compensation or an incentive given by the bank that is going to finance the loan to the mortgage company/loan agent who is doing the loan transaction. The higher the interest rate the loan agent sells to the client, the more rebate the bank will give. This is a topic we will focus on in upcoming chapters.

How this, so-called, free loan is acquired is typically through a higher interest rate. Basically, the loan agent issues the client a higher interest rate, which in turn earns the agent more rebate, which pays for the closing costs "behind the scenes." This is the façade of getting a free deal. The client does not see the fees and therefore believes it to be a *free* loan.

Essentially, the client is financing the fees into the mortgage rate. If a client has fallen victim to this creative way of financing and keeps the loan for a decent amount of time, the costs very well may add up to double what the original closing costs were. It is sad when a company advertises the "NO FEE" loan option. The reality is, a true "No Fee" loan does not exist. You as a client are paying for it one way or another.

In this chapter, "Behind the Scenes Part 1," you are beginning to understand what goes on behind a predatory loan agent's door. You are taking the first step in protecting yourself from predatory lending. These steps of discovery are empowering you to take control of one of the biggest financial investments of your life. It has been said, "Once you experience being in control of your financial future, it really is addictive." Get addicted to educating yourself against this out-of-control problem in the mortgage industry. Allow *UnMasking the Mortgage Madness* to help you distinguish between mortgage myth and your reality.

4

Behind the Scenes Part 2

What a Predatory Loan Agent wants to hide

Predatory Loan Agents will try to mentally and emotionally position you. They will strive to place you in a certain classification and try to convince you that you are only worthy of certain loan programs and interest rates.

One thing my sons Kaleb and Joshua love to do is watch magic shows on television. Whenever they see a magician they always want to stop and watch. I've noticed over the years the illusionists seem to get more and more extreme with their tricks.

I recall one evening as we were watching an illusionist do magic tricks on the streets of New York. My sons were convinced what they were watching was real.

This illusionist was mesmerizing the crowd that was following him. He was putting his hands through storefront windows without getting cut. He would tell people to think of a card and then tell them the very card they were thinking of. The most impressive trick was levitating. It appeared he could make himself float up to six inches. The contagiousness of the crowd's exuberant reaction affected my boys. They too began to outwardly express their awe and wonder at what this illusionist had done.

I began to explain that the gentleman really did not float upward. He made everyone think he had levitated. My kids were convinced I was wrong. Seven-year-old Joshua began to argue with me. He went on and on about how the people who were actually there would have seen the magician's feet on the ground. I explained to him that the trick is strictly about placement. The illusionist places the crowd where he wants them. He then positions himself at a specific angle and instructs the crowd where to look.

Joshua still did not believe me. I told him I knew how to do the trick as well. He laughed at me and went and got his older brother Kaleb to come watch what he thought would be a futile attempt at this trick.

I positioned Kaleb and Joshua where I wanted them. I then moved about eight feet in front of them and angled myself slightly. I instructed them to watch both my heels. The baggy pants I was wearing, hid how I was doing the illusion. I went through all the theatrics and began to "float upward" about four inches. When I was finished, Kaleb and Joshua were speechless for about five seconds. Then they began to scream. I have never laughed so hard. They yelled, "No way! I can't believe it!" Then they asked me to do it again. Of course, I told them I could not because it took too much energy out of me.

After 10 minutes of begging me to tell how I did the trick, I conceded. I again explained how the trick was about positioning and directing. I positioned everyone involved, and then I directed where I wanted their attention. Both of them just laughed and could not believe the simplicity of the trick.

Working with PLAs is very much like Kaleb and Joshua's experience. The PLAs may not physically be able to position you, but they will try to mentally and emotionally position you. They will strive to place you in a certain classification and try to convince you that you are only worthy of certain loan programs and interest rates. At the same time, they will position *themselves* in such a way that they appear to be the only lender in town who can accommodate someone with your specific scenario. One of their goals is to accomplish this manipulation of placement to reach their main objective: to make a handsome profit off their client. When people fall for such illusions they become victims of predatory lending.

Last chapter you learned about **the Bait and Switch, Interest Rate Quoting, and Selling the "NO FEE" loan**. I would like to share with you four other common tricks of the trade that take place behind your typical predatory loan agent's door.

Behind the Scenes Trick #4: *Advertising!*

Remember being in school and having a substitute teacher for the day. There were always students in the class who would push the limits of the substitute. They tested the boundaries to see what they could get away with. Once they crossed over the line, the students identified the boundaries and knew how far they could go.

A lot of those students are business owners today. Unfortunately, they have not outgrown the testing of the boundaries. This time they are not testing the boundaries of a substitute teacher, but are testing the boundaries of the law. They will advertise and push the limits of their advertising to such a degree they are riding the fence line of "false advertising."

I am reminded of a funny story a friend of mine shared with me. Steve was a vice president of a high-end electronics company. They sold televisions, stereos, and complete home theatre systems. He shared one day that the owner of the company wanted to advertise that not only did they have the best quality of electronic equipment, but also the best prices. A few of the management team felt a little odd competing for business with some sort of slogan that communicated *"the lowest price around."* There was a catalog that came out quarterly which had all the advertisements from all the companies in America who sold high-end electronics. This catalog had up to 800 pages. For fun, one of the executives decided to spend a little time going through the catalog to count how many companies claimed to have the lowest price anywhere. Over 400 ads (companies) claimed they had the lowest prices. The executives sat back and laughed as only one of the 400 ads could be true. To not compromise the integrity of their product and who they were, they decided against playing *"the lowest price in town"* game.

The First Amendment grants us the right of free speech and protects all forms of communication, including advertising. However, the U.S. Constitution gives the federal government the power to regulate interstate commerce. Most state constitutions give individual state governments the power to regulate business practices, i.e., advertising, conducted solely within their state.

Congress has passed an act that has the greatest effect on advertising: The Federal Trade Commission (FTC) Act.

According to the Federal Trade Commission, "The FTC Commission is empowered, among other things, to prevent unfair methods of competition, and unfair or deceptive acts or practices in or affecting commerce."

Basically, this Act states that false advertising is a form of unfair and deceptive business practices. The obvious interpretation of "false advertisement" is advertisements that are simply not true.

The FTC Act gives the FTC authority to regulate advertising. They have issued regulations barring advertisements that could be misleading, even if they are true. A famous example involves a major company that is a brand of aspirin. The maker of this aspirin product ran ads claiming that clinical tests showed that their product delivered the same headache relief as the leading pain relief prescription. The ad did not mention that aspirin itself is the leading pain medicine. The FTC determined that the ad was misleading. The ad implied that their company's product was more effective than aspirin, when in fact the product was really just aspirin.

The FTC also has the power to order companies to correct their ads. A famous mouthwash was publicized for years as a cold and sore throat remedy. The FTC forced the manufacturer to run ads stating their product could not cure colds or relieve sore throats.

Mortgage companies are aware that advertising is a very powerful tool. Sometimes they, too, ride the fence line of "false advertising." The number one goal for any company is to make their phone ring. Advertising, when done correctly can accomplish just that.

However, there is a problem in society when it comes to mortgage ads. The bulk of education people receive is through advertising. I can't count how many times I've heard a client say to me, "I heard on the radio," "I was reading in the newspaper," or "How come I can't get a lower rate? This billboard said..." People seem to forget that advertising is a creative vehicle whereby a company will promote their product simply to get customers in the door.

People tend to educate themselves through unrealistic advertising. What is forgotten is those ads are often plays on words. I've heard radio ads communicate: "You too can have this low, fixed-rate mortgage of 1.25%." If the interest rates dropped to a fixed 1.25%, it would be all over the news, and in every paper across America. Typically, there will be a disclaimer on or in the ad. A printed ad will most likely have a disclaimer in a very small font at the bottom of the ad. If it is a radio ad, the disclaimer comes in the form of an audio clip with a voice talking a million miles an hour. Also, the company will say that there is a fixed *portion* of the 1.25% loan program. The reality is, the loan program they are advertising is an adjustable rate mortgage disguised as a fixed-rate mortgage.

When it comes to advertising in the mortgage industry, remember these two things:

1. Mortgage ads can be a cookie cutter product where you have to fit just perfectly into their scenario to qualify.

2. If it seems too good to be true, then it probably is.

Behind the Scenes Trick #5: **Locking Interest Rates!**

The PLA often times will *play the market*. In other words, they'll gamble with your money, through your interest rate. Basically, the PLA will quote an interest rate. If you agree to move forward with the quoted rate, you may be asked if you would like to secure the interest rate by locking it for a 30-day period. The PLA will go on to explain that the lock will protect you in case rates go up. If the rate goes up, you would be secure or "locked" at the lower rate. A lot of times a client will opt to lock the quoted interest rate. However, the PLA *will not lock their rate*. They will wait a few days to see if the rates will go down and if they do, then they will lock the interest rate. It would not necessarily be at the now lower interest rate, but at the higher quoted interest rate from days earlier. Why would they do that? Because they will make more money in "backend rebates," an incentive paid by the bank to the broker/loan agent based on the interest rate sold to the client. Instead of passing on the savings to you, they pocket the benefits for themselves. This is a gamble that goes both ways. If they do not lock the interest rate when agreed and rates go up, you could still lose. The PLA very well could come back to you and make up some excuse as to why they were unable to acquire the earlier quoted interest rate and then issue a higher rate. They were playing the market, gambling if you will, with your money. Later, I will show you what forms to request to safeguard yourself from this experience.

Behind the Scenes Trick #6: **Selling the monthly payment!**

I remember when I bought my first car. It was a 1991 Honda CRX. It only had 14 miles on it. I was really excited. I remember the saleswoman as she went into her sales pitch. She kept referring to the price of the car as a monthly payment. She never spoke to the sticker price, the term of the loan, or the interest rate. Everything was about the monthly payment. She steered my focus off other compensating factors and focused on what would affect my monthly pocketbook. She said "I could get you into this car for $300 a month." I knew I could not afford such a payment. My limit was $225 per month. Being the great negotiator I was, I fired back, "How about $225?" She did the typical, let-me-go-ask-my-manager bit. She had me sit there for about 10 minutes and finally came back. Looking very tired from an apparent negotiation on my behalf, she said, "The best I can do is $235 per month." I felt like I had won, as I got her to come down $65.00. I walked away that day with a smile on my face, but unbeknownst to me, my saleswoman had a bigger smile on her face as my interest rate pushed 15% over a five-year period.

When dealing with PLAs they very well may steer your focus toward your monthly payment. It is a mistake to focus exclusively on the monthly payment. It's not the whole story. There are many other compensating factors that must be considered to make sure you are getting into the best loan program, one that meets not only your short-term needs but long-term goals as well.

You want to pay attention to (refer to glossary for definitions):

- *What is the loan's interest rate?*

- *What is your Annual Percentage Rate (APR)?*

- *Are the regularly scheduled monthly payments going to pay off the loan or is there one large balloon payment at the end?*

- *Is the loan an adjustable rate mortgage? If so, is there a fixed period of time before the interest rate will adjust, and how will it affect the monthly payment once it adjusts? Is there a* life cap *on how much it will adjust? A life cap is the max adjustment the interest rate will increase on a particular ARM. The borrower will not experience the interest rate exceeding past the set life cap.*

- *Are your taxes and insurance included in the monthly mortgage payment?*

If you factor in everything, you will be able to make an educated decision on what loan program best fits your present and future needs.

Behind the Scenes Trick #7: **Selling the golden program!**

Have you ever been forced into something? You went ahead and agreed to do something you felt uncomfortable doing. Maybe your uncomfortable feeling stemmed from knowing the very thing you were getting ready to do was wrong. Maybe there was just uncertainty in the matter and your lack of understanding created anxiety.

When I was 18, I was at my bank cashing my paycheck. I was through with my business and as I was headed for my car, a gentleman in the parking lot who wanted to sell me home theater speakers approached me. He said that he owned a company that did custom installs for homes and when he was at his client's house (earlier that day), the client decided to not purchase all the speakers originally ordered. He showed me what I thought to be the original invoice for the client's order. He took me over to his van, which had a custom install logo on the side of it, where he had six additional speakers. They were brand new and still in their original boxes. The gentleman said he was not in the business of selling speakers, but had unfortunately purchased too many for the job. He wanted to just get rid of them and was not looking to make any money off the deal. He told me he was willing to sell them at cost. He went on to explain he would lose money if he sent them back to the distributor.

His salesmanship went to a whole new level as he saw this wide-eyed 18-year-old boy show interest. He began to brag about the quality of the product. He showed me a glossy flyer, which advertised what the speakers retailed for. He went on and on about what a great deal I would be getting. I was sold. I purchased two of the speakers.

However, to my surprise, when I got home, the speakers I had purchased didn't even match. They were different colors. As for the quality of speakers, they were marginal at best. That was $160 I will never get back.

What happened? I was a victim of salesmanship peer pressure. The salesman spoke well, spoke fast, and spoke to what appealed to me. Although I had a check in my heart about the transaction, I was mesmerized by the deal I was getting. He made me feel I had to have those speakers, and it would be wrong if I passed up that opportunity.

Most of us dealt with peer pressure growing up. Unfortunately, as adults we may still deal with it in our business dealings.

In the mortgage industry it is not uncommon for the PLA to try to steer you into the wrong loan program. Different loans have different structures, terms, features, etc. The predatory loan agent often will match you and your goals incorrectly with a loan program, all the while, highlighting the pros and not the cons of the program. Different programs offer different rates with different ranges of rebate benefits to be made by the loan agent. A PLA may steer you toward a specific program that may enrich the PLA's bottom line, while costing you money.

Never feel pressured into a particular loan program. In a news release at the 2004 Annual Convention, the California Association of Mortgage Brokers (CAMB) released it's official definition of predatory lending.

"Predatory lending is defined as intentionally placing consumers in loan products with significantly worse terms and/or higher costs than loans offered to <u>similarly qualified consumers</u> in the region for the primary purpose of enriching the originator and with little or no regard for the costs to the consumer."

"Getting a loan can be the most important financial transaction in a person's life, and we want to be sure that efforts to deliver the American Dream do not become a nightmare due to dishonest predatory lending practices," CAMB past President Jon Eberhardt said. "With this clear and concise definition of predatory lending, people can protect themselves, and the industry can continue to help consumers become homeowners."

Choosing the right loan program is not just important for your needs, but could save you thousands of dollars in the long run. Acquiring just the right mortgage can be a burdensome process as there are so many different loan programs all with differing interest rates, features, and fees.

Reputable mortgage companies and loan agents will make every effort to make you aware of and comfortable with their loan program options.

We all have the power to choose. Part of our decision-making process should not be based on peer pressure. Choose to not be pressured from friends, family members, and especially sales people.

If you are working with a loan agent who seems to be steering you or pressuring you into a particular direction, pause and ask yourself?

- ***Do the terms of the loan program match my goals?***

If you plan on retiring in your home or staying there for a long period of time, make sure the loan program harmonizes with your plans. An adjustable-rate mortgage may not necessarily be the program of choice, despite the tempting lower monthly payment. If you plan on only keeping the property for a certain period of time such as, three years, five years, seven years, etc., a good adjustable-rate mortgage may be the most cost effective way to go.

- *Does my personal scenario seem as if I may be able to get a better loan than what I am being sold?*

PLAs are known for using your past against you. You may have had bad credit in the past. Maybe even a bankruptcy. Time very well may be your friend, and you are not aware of it. In other words, each loan program has what is called "Guidclines" or "Underwriting Guidelines." These guidelines are used to qualify prospective clients to various loan programs. However, guidelines have been known to change.

You may be able to get the best conforming interest rate on the market with a bankruptcy in your past. At the time of your loan, underwriting guidelines may state that if you have no late payments of any kind after your bankruptcy and your bankruptcy discharge date is over three years old, you *may* qualify for your desired loan program. In the upcoming chapter entitled "Decisions, Decisions, Decisions," you will discover what loan programs may be right for you. You will learn what they are, how they work, and why one would choose them.

At the beginning of this chapter we discussed how PLAs would try to mentally and emotionally position you, the consumer. They will strive to place you in a certain classification to convince you that you are only worthy of certain loan programs and interest rates. The PLA is aware of the fact you do not know about the underwriting guidelines. Therefore, they may try to position or place you emotionally as a disqualified borrower for the conforming interest rates/programs. They will then place you in an unfair loan program with potentially higher interest rates. These programs benefit the PLA and not you.

Remember, not all loan agents operate utilizing the tactics we've discussed in "Behind the Scenes Part 1 and 2." There are tens of thousands of honest loan agents who deserve the professional respect and opportunity to serve good clients. The problem this industry has is there have been loan agents who have abused the mortgage business, which in turn, has unfortunately painted this wonderful industry in a bad light.

Chapter

5

Identifying Your TRUE Costs
Part 1

*Time and time again, the consumer will look at the total
closing costs on their Good Faith Estimate and attribute those
costs directly to their loan agent's pay. It's simply not true.*

About a few weeks before Christmas, my son Jared came across my checkbook. He wasn't meaning to pry, nor was he playing with it. He was just looking at one of the blank checks. I asked him what he was doing. He looked up at me with his big blue eyes and said, "Dad, do these numbers at the bottom of the check show how much money you can spend on Christmas this year?" I laughed. I assured him those numbers were just routing numbers and our checking account number. If I were to be honest, both he and I were disappointed, but more so my son. He simply just misunderstood.

The way my son misunderstood the numbers on the check is similar to the way most consumers misunderstand the numbers regarding their closing costs. Time and time again, the consumer will look at the total closing costs on their Good Faith Estimate and attribute those costs directly to their loan agent's pay. It's simply not true. In the next chapter, "Identifying Your TRUE Costs Part 2," you will learn how to identify junk fees, the true cost of the loan, and where those costs actually go.

This chapter will focus on which charges directly affect your loan agents and their company. Without setting the industry standard, I am going to show you how loan agents are compensated. You will notice when loan agents quote an interest rate, in many cases, they are quoting what dictates their compensation.

If loan agents are working directly with a bank or are employed by a broker, there is one word that ties them together. It's *revenue.* It doesn't matter if the loan agents are salaried employees or paid by commission. *Revenue* is what allows loan agents to receive a paycheck. Salaried employees in most cases are directed by their employers what to charge the client, and those charges define their salary as well as any bonuses they qualify for. A commissioned loan agent typically receives a percentage of the total revenue generated on a loan.

Before you can understand *revenue,* you will need to understand what is "origination" and "rebate."

Origination: The fee charged on the Good Faith Estimate for originating a loan.

Rebate: An incentive paid by the bank to the broker/loan agent based on the interest rate that is sold to the client. The higher the interest rate, the more rebate. Rebate is also known as or referred to as "Yield Spread Premium (YSP)."

Origination + Rebate = *Revenue.* These two charges equal what is often referred to as *"total revenue."* Your loan agent does not receive 100% of the total revenue as income. If your loan agent is a salaried employee, the *total revenue* supports the salary and any bonus due. Commissioned agents receive a **percentage** of the revenue while their company receives the remainder to cover their overhead costs. Typically, those percentages are anywhere from 30% to 80%. Those percentages will differ between banks and brokerages according to their own individual pay scales.

I would like to introduce to you what is known as a Rate Sheet. A Rate Sheet is a chart of interest rates with points, or known in the mortgage world as *prices*. Each point or price is attached to the particular rates located on the chart. The lender/financier prepares the rate sheet. The prices are the rebate benefits to the loan agent or actual costs of buying down the interest rates for the consumer. The prices and/or costs are what the lender is willing to accept at the time the sheet is distributed.

This sample rate sheet is not specific to any bank and/or interest rates. Some rate sheets may differ in appearances; however, their function is similar.

SAMPLE RATE SHEET: *ask to see rate sheet*

30 Year Fixed - Conforming			
Rate	**15-day**	**30-day**	**45-day**
7.625	3.250	3.375	3.500
7.750	2.625	2.750	2.875
7.875	2.125	2.250	2.375
8.000	1.500	1.625	1.750
8.125	0.875	1.000	1.125
8.250	0.375	0.500	0.625
8.375	(0.125)	0.000	0.125
8.500	(0.750)	(0.625)	(0.500)
8.625	(1.250)	(1.000)	(0.875)
8.750	(1.750)	(1.625)	(1.500)
8.875	(2.125)	(2.000)	(1.875)
9.000	(2.500)	(2.375)	(2.125)
9.125	(2.875)	(2.750)	(2.500)
9.250	(3.125)	(3.000)	(2.750)

← Percentages

fictitious interest rates for example only

Here we have four columns:

1. The interest rate column

2. 15-day lock

3. 30-day lock

4. 45-day lock.

The numbers below the lock periods are percentages.

Not always, but typically you would want to lock in your interest rate for 30-days.

Notice the interest rate of 8.375%. On a 30-day lock, it is priced as 0.000 percent. This is known as PAR Pricing or a PAR interest rate in the mortgage industry.

30 Year Fixed - Conforming

Rate	15-day	30-day	45-day	
7.625	3.250	3.375	3.500	
7.750	2.625	2.750	2.875	
7.875	2.125	2.250	2.375	
8.000	1.500	1.625	1.750	
8.125	0.875	1.000	1.125	
8.250	0.375	0.500	0.625	
8.375	(0.125)	0.000	0.125	← PAR Pricing
8.500	(0.750)	(0.625)	(0.500)	
8.625	(1.250)	(1.000)	(0.875)	← 1% Rebate
8.750	(1.750)	(1.625)	(1.500)	
8.875	(2.125)	(2.000)	(1.875)	
9.000	(2.500)	(2.375)	(2.125)	
9.125	(2.875)	(2.750)	(2.500)	
9.250	(3.125)	(3.000)	(2.750)	

fictitious interest rates for example only

PAR Pricing/PAR Interest Rate: The absolute lowest inter-est rate on that particular day, at that particular time, for that particular loan program before technically having to buy down the rate.

Note: PAR Pricing pays zero rebate to the broker/ loan agent.

Usually the clients will not be offered the PAR inter-est rate of 8.375% because there is no rebate to be made on the loan. More than likely, they will be quoted 8.625%. Why? Notice the 30-day lock column. You will see (1.000). Remember, that number is a percentage. Whenever the per-centage number is in parenthesis or has a negative or minus symbol in front {-1.000}, the interest rate, if sold to the client, is paying a rebate to the broker or loan agent. If the percentage number is NOT in parenthesis or does not have a negative or minus symbol in front, then it is the TRUE cost to the client to buy down the interest rate.

Let's do an example:

If the loan amount were $300,000, at 8.625% the loan agent would receive a one-point rebate equaling $3000. If the loan agent were charging a one percent origination on the Good Faith Estimate, then the agent would have earned *total revenue* of $6000 (*not uncommon*).

This is where it can be considered a little unfair. Look at the 9.250% interest rate. Now, look at what the rebate agents would make if they sold their client that interest rate. That is three percentage points. On a $300,000 loan amount, the PLA's rebate is $9000 plus the one percent origination fee, equaling $3000. That is *total revenue* of $12,000. This could be viewed a bit excessive if the client can qualify for the much lower interest rate.

30 Year Fixed - Conforming

Rate	15-day	30-day	45-day	
7.625	3.250	3.375	3.500	
7.750	2.625	2.750	2.875	
7.875	2.125	2.250	2.375	
8.000	1.500	1.625	1.750	
8.125	0.875	1.000	1.125	
8.250	0.375	0.500	0.625	
8.375	(0.125)	0.000	0.125	
8.500	(0.750)	(0.625)	(0.500)	
8.625	(1.250)	(1.000)	(0.875)	1% Rebate
8.750	(1.750)	(1.625)	(1.500)	
8.875	(2.125)	(2.000)	(1.875)	
9.000	(2.500)	(2.375)	(2.125)	
9.125	(2.875)	(2.750)	(2.500)	3% Rebate
9.250	(3.125)	(3.000)	(2.750)	equalling $9000

fictitious interest rates for example only

Pop quiz:

If a client said to the loan agent, "My neighbor just got 8.125% on their 30-year fixed mortgage. Can you get me that interest rate?" What do you think the loan agent might say? In most cases, the agent would look at their rate sheet and say, "Yes, however it is going to cost you, two points."

30 Year Fixed - Conforming

Rate	15-day	30-day	45-day	
7.625	3.250	3.375	3.500	
7.750	2.625	2.750	2.875	
7.875	2.125	2.250	2.375	
8.000	1.500	1.625	1.750	
8.125	0.875	1.000	← 1.125	True Cost "1" Point
8.250	0.375	0.500	0.625	
8.375	(0.125)	0.000	0.125	
8.500	(0.750)	(0.625)	(0.500)	
8.625	(1.250)	(1.000)	(0.875)	
8.750	(1.750)	(1.625)	(1.500)	
8.875	(2.125)	(2.000)	(1.875)	
9.000	(2.500)	(2.375)	(2.125)	
9.125	(2.875)	(2.750)	(2.500)	
9.250	(3.125)	(3.000)	(2.750)	

fictitious interest rates for example only

What does the rate sheet reflect as the true cost to buy down the interest rate to 8.125%?

Technically, the rate sheet calls for a one-point cost to buy down the interest rate to 8.125%. Most loan agents (not predatory loan agents) need to make at least one percent or one point in rebate. There is nothing predatory about making rebate. Making excessive rebate to feed the greed of a loan agent is definitely questionable. In this scenario, many loan agents would tell their clients they would have to pay two-points to buy down the interest rate to 8.125%. The reason is, if they charge their client two-points, then one-point goes to the bank for buying down the desired interest rate, and one-point is credited toward their total revenue. But the reality is, the bank they are taking the loan through is only calling for one-point to be paid for the interest rate of 8.125%.

How can you protect yourself from excessive charging from the PLA? Are there any guidelines or laws that serve you, the consumer? There are mortgage-fee regulations and/or fee compliance protections to help safeguard the consumer.

In 1968, the federal **Truth in Lending Act** (TILA) was originated by Congress, as a part of the Consumer Protection Act. This act was designed to protect consumers in credit transactions from **predatory lenders**. This law necessitates clear disclosure of key terms of the loan transaction and all costs. In 1994, the **Home Ownership and Equity Protection Act** (HOEPA) came about. It added special protections to the Truth in Lending Act (TILA). HOEPA was a response by Congress regarding accounts of abusive lending practices that involve predatory lenders who originated home loans to equity-enriched properties with cash-poor borrowers. A lot of these victims were the elderly, borrowers with marginal to poor credit and sometimes unsophisticated homeowners. The PLA would rely on the enormity of the consumer's equity as a source of revenue.

The HOEPA establishes requirements for certain loans with high rates and/or high fees. The rules for these loans are contained in Section 32 of Regulation Z. These loans are called "Section 32 Mortgages." If a lender charges too many fees, which exceed the Section 32 standards, they are required to issue a Section 32 statement that lets the borrowers know they are being charged more than what is considered normal or fair charging. If the Section 32 statement is not provided before the contract is signed, the purchaser will be able to cancel the contract. Such Acts lean on mortgage institutions to work within certain parameters.

With that being said, someone asked me what the typical percentage of rebates and charges should be on a loan by the lender. It's a tough question to answer. It's hard to gauge what the standard is and what it should be. In my experience I have observed various ways and amounts loan agents go about charging their clients.

When it comes to the origination fee on the Good Faith Estimate, there are typically two options loan agents will choose in charging their client: one option, a fixed dollar amount and the other, a percentage figure. The loan amounts will often determine which option to choose. For instance, one percent origination on a $100,000 loan amount would only be $1000. If the loan agent's rebate was one percent, that is a *total revenue* of just $2000. If the loan agents were on a 50% commission split, they would only make a thousand dollars. They would have to do a lot of loans to make a decent income, comparable to ANY field of work.

What are fair, normal, or typical charges within the mortgage industry? Before we answer that question, keep in mind it requires the same effort to do a $100,000 loan as it does to do a $500,000 loan. Interest rates may be different due to the loan amounts being so small or considered jumbo loans. As far as the process goes, it doesn't matter.

From my observations (not necessarily the standard to which loan agents should be held) smaller loan amounts such as, $100,000 to $250,000 typically have generated a *total revenue* from $3,500 to $5,000. If your loan amount is in that range and the total revenue of your loan falls within those figures, you can feel comfortable knowing your loan agent is operating within what *could* be considered acceptable/fair charging. Larger loan amounts in excess of $250,000 typically generate anywhere from one and half to two percentage points in *total revenue*. One to two percent of the loan amount is acceptable.

Note: If extraordinary circumstances exist, you may very well be charged a little more without it being considered predatory lending. In such cases, you would be paying a fair price for *extra* services rendered. It's important to remember that not every loan is going to be a cookie cutter deal. In other words, some loans require more attention than others. You may need extra help dealing with a past bankruptcy or a foreclosure. Sometimes a loan agent may need to deal with title issues or any judgments that may be against you. You may need your loan agent to help you repair your credit to enable you to qualify for a home loan. These are just a few issues loan agents may need to deal with in order to help you acquire a loan. These issues require **extra** time and effort. It would not be uncommon for your loan agent to charge a little more because of the extra investment of time and paperwork. Here you are paying for expertise, time, and service.

Now, on the contrary, maybe you are one of those clients who comes to the lender and has the perfect scenario. Your credit is stellar, your home is enriched in equity, you have plenty of liquid assets for any cash reserves requirements that may come up, and your job history is remarkably stable. You would be considered a cookie cutter deal. Does this mean one who possesses such a scenario or qualities should obtain a free loan? Is it safe to assume there is no effort put forth by the loan agent therefore no compensation is required? Absolutely not!

There is a cost of doing business with any and all loan transactions. Companies could not stay in business if they worked for free. Maybe your loan transaction is easy and comes with little headaches. However, you still need a professional loan agent who will submit your loan, order title, open escrow, order appraisal (in most cases), and follow your loan through the entire process up to and through funding. Loan agents will communicate to Real Estate Agents, Processors, Underwriters, Doc Drawers (one who prepares your final paperwork to be signed), Funders, Title reps, Title companies, Escrow companies and agents, Appraisers, etc. A good loan agent knows whom to go to and how to make things happen. You cannot accomplish your transaction all by yourself. Nor do you know how to have certain conversations with the various entities involved. You need someone in the know to facilitate a pleasant experience for you. Fair and just charging should still be a factor in your loan. However, make sure your loan agent is being fair with the assessment of time your loan scenario will call for. If you feel your loan is cut and dried and your loan agent is making more of an issue out of your scenario, get a second or third opinion. Be careful to be *completely honest* with all the lenders you choose to get quotes from. When comparing quotes, make sure you're comparing apples to apples.

I want to encourage you to be responsible with this new knowledge. A loan agent making rebate is not a negative issue. Making an excessive rebate to feed the greed of a predatory loan agent at your expense is wrong. I believe it is important for you as a consumer to understand how the process works but also to be fair with your loan agent.

In many cases, it may make sense to take the PAR rate and pay up to "two percentage points" in your origination. Your loan agent can do the math to see if that type of structure makes sense. This chapter puts you in control concerning your interest rate. If you choose to take a higher rate than PAR, then let it be your decision.

Chapter

6

Identifying Your TRUE Costs
Part 2

*Being taken advantage of is never a good thing.
You feel manipulated, lied to, and sometimes silly. If only we
could see the future, we would better safeguard ourselves
against these experiences.*

One evening when I was 18, I made a run to the store. It was about seven o'clock. When leaving the store, a boy not more than 13 years old stopped me. He began to explain how he lost his wallet and had been asking people all day if they could spare some money so he could buy his bus ticket to go back to his aunt's house in Phoenix, Arizona. He showed me some ones and fives and said he was about twenty dollars short. He said he had about an hour before the last bus left town. Feeling sorry for the boy and knowing the bus station was right around the corner, I gave him the twenty dollars he needed. What made for a smooth transaction was his timing. His story was believable, and I was gullible. The boy ran off in the direction of the bus station. An employee of the store I just shopped at approached me. He asked me what I was doing. I shared this young boy's story and what I had done. He just shook his head. He went on to explain, how this kid is a panhandler and he constantly is asked to leave the store. Instantly I was furious. I got back into my car. However, it was too late. The boy was gone and could not be found.

Being taken advantage of is never a good thing. You feel manipulated, lied to, and sometimes silly. If only we could see the future, we would better safeguard ourselves against these experiences. The twenty dollars I lost that evening is a drop in the bucket compared to the monies lost on the Good Faith Estimates predatory lenders issue their clients.

I cannot show you the future; however, I can equip you with certain signs to watch for when dealing with lenders concerning this often-misunderstood document known as a Good Faith Estimate.

What is the **G**ood **F**aith **E**stimate (GFE)?

Good Faith Estimate: An estimate of all closing fees including pre-paid and escrow items as well as lender charges.

This document must be given to the borrower within *three* days after submission of a loan application.

In this chapter, I will give you insight about your GFE. You'll learn what to expect concerning the GFE, what fees to look for, and how to identify true junk fees.

Remember these three things when dealing with any lender:

1) *Request a copy of your Good Faith Estimate early on.*

When establishing a relationship with a lender, one of the first items to request is a copy of the GFE. If you have asked for one and your loan agent cannot seem to get you one right away (at least within 24 hours), that is a red flag! Your lender has the ability to produce this document immediately and is supposed to by the Real Estate Settlement Procedures Act (RESPA). If not, your lender very well may be out of RESPA compliance.

2) *You want to see numbers instead of letters on your Good Faith Estimate.*

If you see codes in your estimate where there should be numbers, that is a red flag. You may see "PFC" on a particular line item. PFC stands for Prepaid Finance Charge. These charges are fees that affect your APR. A lender has the ability to figure the estimated dollar amount (fees) per line item. By doing so, it offers you a better understanding of what your total closing costs will be. As the client, you should know this document is just an estimate. However, this estimate should be given with *figures* not *letters*. With that being said, there is a code such as P.O.C. that might surface on the GFE. P.O.C. stands for Paid Outside of Closing. If you pay for your appraisal up front and will not be including the appraisal fee in your closing cost, P.O.C. may then be applied. Also, per Housing of Urban Development (HUD), the charges shown on the GFE must include any payments by the lender to affiliate or independent parties. These payments should be shown as P.O.C. All P.O.C.s will be accompanied by a dollar figure as well. Typically, the dollar figures are bracketed. If the lender claims they cannot produce these figures, it is time to change lenders.

3) *Request ALL closing costs, not just the lender's.*

When inquiring about closing costs, if the lender tells you only about their lending fees and leads you to believe the cost of the loan is a certain origination percentage, that is red flag as well. You have not been informed of all the third party fees that are *naturally* part of the loan. What if you want your taxes and insurance in your mortgage payment? You'll need to include those costs as well.

Lenders know all the answers to your questions. They may give you a short answer to appease you. The reality is, there is more to know than a short answer. If working with a PLA, the client will usually discover the reality of the closing costs in the eleventh hour.

You want to choose a lender who will disclose all the fees charged at the beginning of the loan process. A lender who is forthright with you in the beginning allows you to make an educated decision. That type of lender deserves your business.

When acquiring a loan, how do you know if you are paying a fair and just price for services rendered? The GFE form itself is foreign to most people. The form's format may change between banks. Even if the GFE form looks different between banks, they should still communicate the general costs of the loan (see sample form in Chapter Nine). You will have to acclimate yourself to this document. Once you get your bearings on what it is you are reading, the challenge becomes to identify what should or (maybe) should not be on the form. The GFE is a playground for the PLAs. They can easily manipulate it and sell you on costs that are simply untrue.

One thing that drives my wife crazy is my dresser "junk" drawer. She accuses me of being a pack rat. The top of my dresser has two small drawers side by side. These drawers are not meant for clothing. They are more for small items such as keys, wallets, loose change, etc. One day my wife opened these two drawers to put something in there. She was appalled. She did not see keys, a wallet, or loose change. She saw what she would refer to as junk, stuff I should have thrown away or found a more appropriate home for. She found a hammer, kite string (we don't even own a kite), a guitar tuner, phone cords, shower curtain rod hangers, papers from meetings over two years old, chap stick, balloons, hair brushes, dental floss, small booklets, etc.

I'll never forget the look on her face. It was a look of disbelief. She asked me if this was a joke. I assured her it was not. I explained that a man needs to have a junk drawer. Plus, who knows when I might buy a kite and need some string? She looked at me and rolled her eyes.

What made me proud was when my eldest son Kaleb got his first, what we called, "big boy" dresser. One day Tiffany opened his top dresser drawer (which was actually meant for clothes) and found that Kaleb had converted it into a junk drawer. When asked, "What is all this junk?" He replied, "Daddy has a junk drawer." She just laughed. Kaleb actually thought it was normal to have such a drawer.

My junk drawer is a great visual of the Good Faith Estimates that many clients receive. They are just filled with various junk (fees). There are fees that just do not belong, fees that do nothing more than clutter the Good Faith Estimate. What is unfortunate is many consumers are like my son. They read their GFE and assume what they are seeing is normal and therefore accept it. The problem is, when dealing with a predatory loan agent, they run the risk of additional fees, which in turn, are a greater unnecessary cost.

Some lenders are accused of having a junk drawer. The problem is their junk drawer is not found in a dresser but in the GFE they issue their clients. They take what is known as junk fees and cram them throughout the GFE to increase their revenue. The term "Junk Fee" is basically a slang term for the extra fees the would-be predatory lender puts on the GFE. These fees are usually outside the normal lender fees and described in very official language. These junk fees are supposed to reimburse the lender for specific expenses. The real purpose is to enhance the PLA's bottom line.

Note: *This is not to say that a lender does not have high costs in originating a loan.*

Due to the many parties involved in the loan who are compensated, the PLAs feel they can take advantage of the client's confusion and tack on additional costs. They believe they can extract more dollars from the borrower through these added, often unnecessary fees. It's selfish, and it lacks integrity.

This is my definition of **INTEGRITY:**

Doing what is best for someone else, when another decision would be best for you.

When it comes to predatory lending, it is all about making a decision that is best for the loan agent and not for the client. Unfortunately, the majority of the predatory loans are perpetrated upon sub-prime clients, because of the PLAs and their practices. They will try to take advantage of a client who is desperate for a loan or who cannot qualify for an "A" paper deal due to poor credit or an unusual loan scenario. This type of poor lending practice has effected the sub-prime industry and tarnished it's name. If you are a client who must go down the sub-prime road for one reason or another, do not be afraid. It does not mean you will be taken advantage of. I have a friend named Peter who works for a wholesale sub-prime bank in Southern California. He would be considered a "sub-prime wholesale rep." There are sub-prime banks, such as the one Peter works for, that have the borrower's best interest in mind. In other words, if there is no benefit to the borrower, the sub-prime bank will reject the file. Peter and his team have been known to reject a file because there was no benefit to the borrower. Here's a scenario he and his team came upon. They ensured that the only benefit was going to the borrowers and not to the loan agent.

A loan agent had a client for whom he did a loan. The loan was fine and desirable for the borrower at the time of closing. The loan agent was paid fairly, and even hand-somely, for the service he had performed. The borrower was extremely satisfied concerning the service and care received.

Unbeknownst to the borrowers, life threw them an unforeseen curveball one month after the closing of their loan. The borrowers found themselves faced with a large, unexpected, cash need. Understandably, they turned to their home for rescue. One problem, banks do not like repeat business, as odd as that may seem. Repetitive refinances are bad for borrowers, bad for equities, and are indicative of predatory lending, and fraud schemes. Banks do not like the idea of a broker/loan agent milking borrowers for repeti-tive fees, at the expense of their loan balance. However, in this case, the borrowers' need was legitimate, urgent, and *verified*. Peter's bank wanted to lend them the money to help fulfill what was believed to be a genuine need. Their new (now current lender) would not qualify the borrowers for a new loan. Because of the cash they were now going to get out of the refinance, and the fact that the new loan amount was too close to their value, they were no longer eligible to receive the same type of loan they had just refinanced into. Beside the fact, they had just refinanced a month earlier. Peter's bank was able and willing to do the deal, however, with one demand: the broker was not allowed to charge the borrower *ANY* further fees. The way Peter and his team saw it, the benefit to the borrower from receiving this loan was going to be outweighed by the cost. More practically, since the borrowers had just closed a loan with this loan agent one month earlier, the loan agent already had a complete and accurate loan file. Therefore, they were not going to have to perform more than a bare minimum of work on behalf of this second transaction. The borrower was being helped, Peter's bank was confident they had done the right thing, and the loan agent, though mildly annoyed in the short term, now had a loyal client for life. It worked out for everyone. Fees are a way of life, nobody gets anything for free, and you get what you pay for, but the point is to keep the playing field fair.

There are banks and teams of people who are looking out for the best interest of the client. Conforming, Alt-A, or Sub-prime banks are not in the business of taking advantage their clients. There are financial institutions that have quality reps, such as Peter and his team, who are there and act as a safeguard to the client, especially, in moments where a PLA is being what would be considered unethical.

PLAs can very easily decide to charge above and beyond the normal fees to benefit their bottom line or keep your best interest in mind and charge a fair and just price for the services rendered.

Junk fees are disguised in unfamiliar terminology. Your loan agent knows you are unfamiliar with the industry, and a dishonest loan agent may take advantage of your ignorance. The PLAs are confident if they can label a fee in technical language and come up with a persuasive explanation for the charge, the average client will accept the fee.

Here is a list of past junk fees PLAs have used on their clients. This list is not all-inclusive, but will give you a good idea of what they are and what to look out for:

- Affiliate Consulting fee
- Amortization fee
- Bank Inspection fee
- Lender's Inspection fee
- Settlement fee
- Sign-up fee
- Endorsement fee
- Photograph fee
- Lender's Attorney fee
- Administrative fee (especially if there is already an Underwriting fee)
- Translation fee

My favorite is the "Regulatory Inspection fee." Here is how this fee could be explained:

"You know, Mr. Smith, earlier this year, Fannie Mae and Freddie Mac issued a memo that banks are now required to have a quality control department. Due to all the predatory lending that has taken place during the refinance boom, they are mandating that lenders tighten up their practices, and these QC departments are there to regulate the costs and lending practices of the loan agents. Unfortunately, the *Regulatory Inspection* fee is about $578, but it is truly there to protect you."

Sounds logical right? This explanation is very believable to consumers, especially if they are unfamiliar with the home purchasing process. The problem is, there is no such thing as a *Regulatory Inspection* fee. PLAs know if they can make something sound good and important enough, you may buy into it. If you fall for such schemes, you will be charged a little more in your closing costs. It's tragic.

So, when you receive your Good Faith Estimate, what fees should you see?

There is something you should understand before I explain what are typical or normal fees one would see on a GFE. Closing costs vary widely from state to state, county to county, and even bank to bank. Your residency may determine what you will have to pay. Some banks will term fees differently. The number one example is the Underwriting fee. Some banks call the Underwriting fee an Administrative fee.

When it comes to junk fees, the bottom line is, no fee is a junk fee if the charge is a "service" related fee. In other words, you should pay for services rendered. The Underwriting fee has been labeled as a junk fee. An online search for mortgage junk fees will show that the Underwriting fee seems to make it on some lists. I personally do not feel a *true* Underwriting fee is a junk fee. Just about every loan has to go through an Underwriter. The Underwriter is a human being who actually performs many tasks. This human being would like to get compensated for those efforts.

Here is an idea of what some of the Underwriter's responsibilities are:

The Underwriters approve or deny mortgage loans by following mortgage standards and guidelines. They review and evaluate information on mortgage loan documents to determine if buyer, property, and loan conditions meet establishment and government standards. They request additional information from the borrowers for qualification purposes. They assemble documents in loan files, including acceptance or denial, and return files to the originating mortgage loan office. They may be authorized by a federal agency to certify that mortgage loan applicant and property.

If you had this job responsibility, wouldn't you want your company to be compensated so they, in turn, could compensate you?

What are normal or widely accepted mortgage fees?

There are three sets of fees you should expect:

1. Lender/Broker Fees

2. Third Party Fees

3. Impounds/Interest

Lender/Broker Fees

Lender/Broker fees are charged by the lender/broker for services rendered. The fees are typically (but not limited to) an Origination, Processing, and Credit report.

Third-Party Fees

The lender for services provided by outside companies collects what is known as third-party fees. They are adding the fees as the other companies work on files and provide a service to the borrower. Your lender does not keep these fees. Here are some of your customary third-party fees:

1. Appraisal

2. Tax Service

3. FEMA

4. Documentation

5. Underwriting

6. Wire Transfer

7. Flood Certificate

8. Escrow

9. Title

10. Recording

11. Discount

12. Notary fees

Impounds and Days of Interest

Impounds and Days of Interest charges are the third set of fees you should expect to see on your Good Faith Estimate. Your impound account is also known as your Escrow or Reserve account. This is not a charge from the lender. If you elect to have your taxes and insurance included in your mortgage payment, the bank will require you to set up a reserve account. They will expect a certain amount of months collected up front for property taxes and hazard (homeowners) insurance.

If your property taxes are $200/month, for example, the bank may require six months' reserves to be collected from you. That is a total of $1200 that will be added to your closing costs. Your loan agent receives no benefit from this cost; this is completely at your discretion and for your convenience. Most banks will allow clients to opt out and not have their taxes and insurance included in their mortgage payment. By doing so, it will lower your *overall* closing costs.

The Days of Interest is a charge based on the day during the month that you close the loan. I had a client in Seattle ask me when her first mortgage payment would be due. We looked at the calendar together and figured what day of the month we would be closing on her loan. We decided January 15 would be the target date. I explained her first mortgage payment would be March 1. She made an interesting comment, "Wow, I get to live in my house for the first six weeks for free!" I explained she was actually going to pay for at least two weeks of that six-week period in her closing costs. It was in the line item of *Days of Interest* on her GFE.

I clarified: if clients closed their loan in a 30-day month on the 20th of that month, they would have 10 days of interest to pay to the new lender. Again, the loan agent does not benefit from this cost. If they closed on the fifth of the month, they would have to pay an estimated 25 days of interest. What you have to realize is you will always pay the remainder of the month's interest no matter what day of the month you close your loan. Some loan agents will target the closing of their client's loan more toward the end of the month. This will potentially save their client a few hundred dollars in total closing costs.

What can you do to better safeguard yourself from being a victim of junk fees? Here is a Good Faith Estimate cheat sheet. You need to understand this sheet is JUST A GUIDE. It is not law. Fees will differ among brokers, banks, and third party companies, as well as between states. This cheat sheet serves as a general guide for what to expect the normal closing costs should be on your Good Faith Estimate. You may find additional charges, *which may be valid*; however, I would advise you to inquire about the purpose of any and all additional charges. Those additional charges very well may be true junk fees. This cheat sheet is not formatted for government loans (FHA/VA), but it is a good guide for conforming/conventional loans and any sub-prime loan.

Closing Costs Cheat Sheet

GFE LINE ITEM	CHARGE	AVERAGE AMOUNT
801	Origination	Up to 2% if you are receiving PAR pricing (i.e., the lowest interest rate)
802	Discount Point	Charged to clients ONLY if they are buying down their rate
803	Appraisal Fee	Varies w/ appraiser and type of appraisal
804	Credit Report	Typically should be no more than $125
809	Tax Servicing Fee	Could be up to $90
810	Processing Fee	Varies w/ lender/broker, could be up to $600
811	Underwriting Fee	Varies w/ bank. Could be up to $1000
812	Wire Transfer Fee	Varies, typically $35
813	Flood Certificate	Typically $13
814	Admin. Fee	Typically charged if no underwriting is charged
824	Rebate	Broker by law discloses rebate on this line
901	Days of Interest	Varies depending on the date of closing
903	Insurance Premium	Only for purchases
1001	Hazard Insurance	Reserve deposit, dictated on closing of loan
1004	Property Tax	Reserve deposit, dictated on month of 1st mortgage payment
1101	Escrow Fee	Varies on escrow company and loan amount/purchase price
1106	Notary Fee	Varies on Notary. Typically $150 - $200
1108	Title Fee	Varies on title company and loan amount/purchase price
1201	Recording Fee	Typically $75

Please see reverse side for instruction

A gentleman who lives in Nashville, Tennessee, was refinancing his $600,000 home. He has a friend who lives in Federal Way, Washington, who is a real estate investor. The gentleman called his friend to let him know he was refinancing his home, and because his friend was familiar with the buying and selling process, he asked him to review his Good Faith Estimate. Unbeknownst to him, the investor had reviewed a segment of the *UnMasking the Mortgage Madness* video presentation, which dealt with the GFE. He was familiar with the Good Faith Estimate Cheat Sheet. He told him he would love to review his paperwork for him, in light of what he had learned through the video. After reviewing his Good Faith Estimate, he noticed a charge of $600 that seemed to be out of place. He counseled his friend to inquire about what looked like an extra fee. The gentleman in Nashville called his loan agent and said, "The Good Faith Estimate looks good. However, I am curious to know what this $600 fee is?" The loan agent stammered in his answer, "Oh, don't worry about that. We can waive that fee for you." A $600 savings just like that.

Watch your Good Faith Estimate carefully. Be sure what you are being charged are necessary, real fees. Utilize this cheat sheet as a guide. With all the numbers and figures that come with this document, this cheat sheet will help you narrow down your questions while trying to discover the true cost of your loan. Do not let the pressures of the PLA force you into paying for unnecessary fees. Do not be paranoid, but guard yourself. If you do not understand what a fee is, you have the right to ask about it; the charge may be legitimate. Remember, if you do not ask, you may not be as lucky as the gentleman from Tennessee.

Chapter

7

Asking the Right Questions the Right Way

In good communication, good questions are being asked. George Bernard Shaw comments, "The single biggest problem in communication is the illusion that it has taken place."

Communication is key in any relationship. What is communication? According to the Encarta® World English Dictionary, it is the exchange of information between individuals by means of speaking, writing, or using a common system of signs or behavior. If there is one thing in life that is the common denominator in anything we do, it is communicating. It doesn't matter if you are actively participating in a sport, your workplace, personal relationships, or any business dealings. Communication will be key to your success.

Take baseball, for example. If you are a pitcher, you have to be communicating to your catcher the pitches you want to throw. If the catcher thinks the pitcher is going to throw the ball high and outside, the catcher will get in a position to react to such a pitch. However, if the pitcher decides to throw low and inside, but does not let the catcher know, that is a recipe for disaster.

In your workplace, your company's success depends on effective communication among staff, clients, and the various levels of management. If people cannot communicate their expectations clearly and properly, how can they expect them to be met?

Our personal relationships hinge on communication. The greatest lesson I've learned about communication has come through my marriage. I have been married for 14 years, but I still feel at times I am learning how to communicate with my wife. Bill Cosby puts it well, "Men and women belong to different species, and communications between them is still in its infancy." Women want their men to feel what they are feeling. Apparently, that is the key for us men to truly understand anything. However, men would desire their wives to be more logical, which would help in their understanding.

Communication breakdown is often the culprit in marital problems. Speaking to the men, nine times out of ten it is not what we are communicating that causes friction with our spouses, but *how* we are communicating. It is more about how we articulate the thoughts we're trying to convey.

In *good* communication, good questions are being asked. The problem we have at times, especially in our business dealings, is asking the *right* questions the *right* way. A lot of times, we may ask questions, but they are the wrong questions or the wrong phrasing. Sometimes we know things are not right but we really don't know how to articulate our thoughts clearly to get the answers we're searching for.

When applying for a home loan, miscommunication is especially dangerous. So dangerous, it has cost clients thousands of unnecessary dollars in their closing costs. Lack of understanding of how to ask the right questions the right way has allowed clients to agree to acquire loan programs that were not a good fit for them. Those loan programs have cost clients tens of thousands of dollars in mortgage payments and/or equity.

When going through the home financing process, there are three categories people would place themselves into:

1) The Seasoned Homeowner

These are individuals who have bought many homes in the past, an investor of residential real estate, or one with many rental homes. These types of individuals feel they have a grasp of what to expect. They are confident and comfortable asking what they perceive to be proper questions.

2) The Inexperienced/First-Time Homeowner

The majority of the public would place themselves in this category. Some of these individuals have never bought a home; therefore, everything is foreign to them. Some may be current or former homeowners. However, since it has been a long time in dealing with a lender, it feels brand new to them. It is very common for these people to feel confused. They do not fully understand what is going on. They ask questions but feel like the answers are going over their head.

3) The Real Estate Professional

These are primarily people in the real estate industry, i.e., real estate agents and brokers. Not all, but a lot of real estate agents feel they have a grasp of how the mortgage industry works. They feel confident they posses enough knowledge to protect their clients and themselves from being taken advantage of by a predatory loan agent. They too, are confident and comfortable asking what they *perceive* to be the proper questions.

It's critical when it comes to asking the right questions the right way. Unfortunately, many PLAs will take advantage of your ignorance in their field of expertise. They will use your lack of knowledge against you. Doctors, lawyers, engineers, and even seasoned real estate agents have asked the wrong questions when applying for a loan. These people are very smart by nature. However, they have not been thoroughly educated about the mortgage industry and how it works. They ask what perceivably would be good questions. In spite of their natural brilliance, they asked the wrong question the wrong way, and their lender took advantage of them.

There are five questions commonly asked by clients. Regrettably, these questions are asked incorrectly. There is a more specific way to ask them, a way that it will cause your loan agent to be honest and ethical with you.

Here are five common questions clients ask, but ask incorrectly:

1) WRONG QUESTION: What are my closings costs?

CORRECT QUESTION: What are my *TOTAL* closing costs? (i.e., all lender fees, third party fees, and impound account costs.)

On occasion, my wife will send me to the grocery store. She will give me a list of all the desired items. When I approach the cashier, like everyone else, I put all my groceries on the belt and wait for the cashier to ring up everything. Now, what good would it be to me if she rang up two-thirds of my groceries and then quoted me my cost? It does me no good to know what my partial costs are. The figure the cashier would quote me would be useless. I do not want to know what two-thirds of my grocery bill would equate to. I want to know the *total* cost of my groceries.

Just as crazy as it would be for a cashier to try to do something like that, PLAs do it all the time with their prospective clients. They have a tendency to not fully answer, "What are my closing costs?" Their fear is if you hear the complete (real) estimated total, it will scare you away. The PLAs feel they run the risk of losing your business. When asked about the closing costs, as a lender, I know exactly what the clients are asking. They want to know the whole financial picture. Often the PLAs will quote just *their* fees and later tack on the remaining true cost of the loan. This way, they get you in the door and involved in the process, so involved, when the real closing costs come into play, you feel tricked and trapped at the same time. With persuasive language, the PLA explains away everything and the loan continues. That is why I suggest you work with a lender who is honest from the beginning.

Be more specific when asking this most common question. The more specific you are with your questions, the more specific you make your loan agent be with the answers.

2) WRONG QUESTION: How many points do you charge?

CORRECT QUESTION: What is your Origination Fee? Are you charging me "Discount points" to buy down my interest rate?

The difference between the "Origination Fee" and the "Discount Point" is widely misunderstood. The PLAs will take advantage of your misunderstanding and use it to their advantage when it comes to selling a loan. Too many people will ask how many "points" are going to be charged. The truth is they do no understand fully what they are asking. It is not your fault, as you have been falsely educated through random ads. Radio ads, television ads, and printed ads seem to use the language of "points." Do not use the language of random ads as a form of communication. If consumers want their loan agents to answer this question correctly, ask them in the language they are accustomed to using with their co-workers behind the scenes. This way, it prevents the would-be predatory loan agent from using your lack of knowledge against you.

Remember the difference between the "Origination" and "Points" also known as "Discount Points."

Origination: The fee charged by the lender/loan agent to originate the loan.

Points (Discount Points): A fee charged to buy down the interest rate.

When asked by a client, "How many points do you charge?", nine times out of ten the loan agent will say, "None." True points or discount points do not go to the loan agent. Discount points are charges from the bank that is initially financing your mortgage. Asking this question the correct way is valuable, as PLAs will often quote a low interest rate to get your business. A client would agree to do business because of this low quote. The PLA counts on you falling for such quotes without fully educating you on how they are able to obtain such a low rate.

The discovery of this scam typically comes during the review of the GFE. You will notice the Discount Point field on the GFE will have a dollar figure that definitely adds to the total closing costs. You will learn your loan agent is having you buy down your interest rate. When questioned, the PLAs will always have a plan "B." They will say you do not have to buy down the interest rate. They will offer various other (higher) rates, much the same as what the other lenders quoted you when you were comparing interest rates. The problem is the PLA used manipulation to get your business while the other lender was being fair and honest, yet *lost* your business. Good lenders will not use such tactics. They may offer you the option to buy down your rate, but never manipulate you into doing so.

If you are going to buy down the rate, that decision needs to be executed by you. Your honest lender can figure out if buying down the interest rate would be cost-effective for you. Ask this question the correct way and you may save yourself time and money!

3) WRONG QUESTION: What is the lowest interest rate I can get?

CORRECT QUESTION: What is today's "PAR" interest rate for the loan program I qualify for?

When loan agents are quoting an interest rate, more than likely they are receiving some sort of rebate from the bank. Remember, rebate is an incentive paid by the bank to the broker/loan agent based on the interest rate sold to the client. I'm not suggesting there is anything wrong with making rebate. However, you do need to be aware, as it may help you decide on an interest rate and cost that will work for you.

People seem to ask what is the lowest rate they can get. That is the wrong question to ask. As brilliant as most people are, they ask this question the wrong way. It allows the loan agents to be subjective. Loan agents can say whatever they want. If they feel like only offering you 6.500% when the rates are at 6.000%, they will. The PLAs justify it by saying, "That is the lowest I *choose* to offer the client. Therefore it is the lowest interest rate that is available to them." That is not the actual lowest interest rate, but unfortunately for that particular client it is.

By asking this question using "mortgage language," it forces the PLA or loan agent to be truthful. You want to ask the question this way, "What is today's PAR interest rate for the loan program I qualify for?" The PAR interest rate (or sometimes referred to as PAR pricing) is the absolute lowest interest rate clients can receive on that particular day without technically having to buy their rate down. If this question is asked in this specific way, it makes the loan agent answer correctly. The "PAR" interest rate cannot be subjective. Par is Par. It's that simple.

The PAR interest rate offers *no rebate* to the lender. If you want the PAR interest rate and are willing to pay a higher origination fee, how do you know that you are truly getting a PAR rate? Because your loan agent said so?

Where's the proof? There are one of two key documents you can request. If you feel your loan agent is not being honest with you, you can always request a copy of the rate sheet. However, that does not mean the loan agent will be able to give you one. It depends on the bank handling your loan. It's still worth inquiring, but some rate sheets do state right on them:

"Intended for use by licensed real estate professionals only; not for public distribution to the consumer."

Most banks have what are called search engines. These search engines are computer programs specific to the bank that have basic built-in guidelines to help a loan agent price out a loan (*figure out the interest rates*) for a client. These search engines are not loan approvals or a commitment to fund the client's loan. Every loan is subject to credit approval, various compensating factors, and "full" underwriting guidelines and process. The loan agent will input your scenario into this computer program, and the program selects the interest rate off the rate sheet for them. Most of the programs are designed to email their findings that usually state if the loan agent is earning any rebate. This sheet should also show if you are paying a discount point for your interest rate. It's a great substitute for the rate sheet.

If you should have the opportunity to preview the rate sheet your loan agent is quoting from, here is what to look for:

PAR pricing will have 0.000 or 100.000 in the lock columns.

Your understanding of what PAR pricing is helps you choose the right interest rate. It puts the control back into your hands and lets you choose. In some cases, it may make sense to choose the PAR rate. A good loan agent can help you decide what is best.

4) WRONG QUESTION: Can you lock my interest rate?

CORRECT QUESTION: Will you lock my interest rate and provide me with a copy of the Lock Confirmation Sheet?

Another key document to request is a Lock Confirmation Sheet. All lenders receive it or some sort of document that shows the bank recognizing that your interest rate has been secured.

Here are other similar documents providing the same information.

- Lock Certificate

- Commitment Letter

- Copy of the Approval

In Chapter One we discussed the difference between the "A" paper world and the Sub-Prime world. I explained an "A" paper client means you have good credit and your loan scenario qualifies for what is considered conforming or "A" paper rates. Conforming loans give clients the option to *lock* their loan. However, if you have poor credit or your loan scenario does not conform to the Fannie Mae or Freddie

Mac guidelines, you very well may need what is known as a sub-prime loan. *Rarely* does sub-prime banking offer any lock opportunities. If you are a sub-prime candidate, you will want to ask for a copy of the Approval or get a Commitment Letter that will show you the exact interest rate you are acquiring. You can often get this document before you sign your final paperwork.

Why is it so important to have these documents? They reveal exactly what you are getting. The Lock Confirmation, Lock Certificate, Commitment Letter, or Approvals typically reveal these items:

- The date the loan was locked

- The date the loan was approved, if you're a sub-prime client

- Your interest rate

- Any *rebates* being made by the loan agent

These documents reveal two important facts, whether you are truly getting the PAR rate your loan agent has promised, and information about your lock. Why is that important? If a PLA asks you if you would like to lock your loan on the 15th of the month, but your lock confirmation shows the lock date to be the 23rd of the month, the PLA very well may have been playing the market at your expense. The Lock Confirmation, Lock Certificate, Commitment Letter, or Approvals are worth gold to your loan agent. If your loan agent claims to have secured your interest rate, there should be one of these documents. These documents are usually the only confirmation from the bank regarding any rebate the agent may be making. If the lender tells you there is no such paperwork, I would question the validity of the loan proposal.

5) WRONG QUESTION: Do you offer a "No-Fee" loan?

CORRECT QUESTION: Can I finance my fees into my interest rate?

There is no such thing as a free lunch! When a lender is advertising a no-fee loan, it usually means you are receiving a higher interest rate. The extra rebate being made through the higher interest rates is being used to pay for your closing costs. You are still paying for the loan; however, you are doing it by way of a higher interest rate. Basically, you are financing your fees into your rate.

In rare cases it may make sense to finance this way. Especially if you are not going to be in your home long-term. If you are planning to keep your loan for a while, your "NO FEE" loan may cost you double if not triple what your actual closing costs might have been. In most cases it is more cost effective to pay your fees up front while taking the lower rate or PAR rate. Do not be a poor steward of your money. Factor in all possibilities regarding paying closing costs. A good loan agent can help you weigh the costs to make an educated decision.

Communication is key. When communicating, it is vital you're on the same page. Part of being on the same page is making your requests clear, and it's often not what you are asking but how you are articulating your questions. I love George Bernard Shaw's quote regarding communication, "The single biggest problem in **communication** is the illusion that it has taken place."

If you will ask these five correct questions, you will find you have lessened the risk of a predatory loan agent taking advantage of you. You owe it to yourself to be well informed about your home financing. The best way to be well informed is to ask the right questions the right way!

8

Decisions, Decisions, Decisions

Which Loan Program is Right for Me?

Which loan program is for me? Before choosing a loan program, identify your goals concerning your home. Once you know where you want to go, you can choose the loan program that will best take you there.

As I grow older, I am more convinced that setting goals in life is necessary to any success I may achieve. A goal is simply the end result of what we want to achieve. Goals can be a destination or an accomplishment. Les Brown said, "Your goals are the road maps that guide you and show you what is possible for your life."

When I was in the sixth grade, our school district put on what was known as the Junior Olympics. The eight area schools would gather their fastest and most athletic fifth and sixth graders. The schools would all compete in various track and field events at the local high school.

One of the events I was going to compete in was the 880 relay. The 880 relay race required four runners per team. The teams would position their runners in two locations around the track that wrapped around the football field. Each runner would run half way around the track where the other runner would be waiting to receive the baton. Once all four runners had run their portion of the race, the meet was over.

I remember one day telling my dad I wanted my group to win this particular race. He asked me if we had set any goals. I didn't know what he meant. All I knew was what I wanted the end result to be. He explained that when you set out to achieve something, you are basically setting a goal. But that is not enough. You have to plan the course properly to reach the desired destination. One must set smaller goals along the way. As we achieve the small goals, we move closer to achieving the main goal.

I got with my teammates and we timed our race to identify how we were doing. We then figured out what our time should be in order to have a chance at winning. The only way to increase our time was to train over the next couple of months. The last recess of every day we would run. When we got home from school, we all committed to run around our neighborhoods. Everything we did was run, run, and run. Before we knew it, our time was getting faster and faster.

I remember the day of the meet. We positioned ourselves around the track. I was the second runner. The gun went off and the runners began their sprint. I noticed something as our first runner, Gene, was beginning the race. He was in dead last! I thought to myself, "Gene is not setting me up for a good run." He was the last one to get to the second runner.

I remember my dad telling me to stay focused and keep my eyes forward and run hard if I was not in the lead. I most certainly was not in the lead at the beginning of my leg of the race. I took off running and gave it all I had. Something amazing happened. I started to catch up to the first runner, then the second, and the third. As I was coming around the corner there was only one runner left to catch. I ran as I'd never run before. By the time I handed the baton off to our third runner I had caught up to the runner who was in first place.

The end result of that meet was Park View Elementary School placed second in the 880 relay. Believe it or not, we met our goal. Yes, our goal was to win, but also to get our run time down. Even though we came in second, we beat our goal time we set for ourselves at the beginning of our training.

My dad said because we set and met our little goals along the way, we as a team experienced the taste of a great race and beat our old running time. We felt we achieved our goal that day.

We set goals in life in just about everything we do. If your goal is to own a home one day, your loan program should play a part in achieving that goal. Not every loan program is the best program. Different programs offer different benefits to the homeowner. You need to ask yourself, "What are my goals concerning my future in this home, and what loan program will help me get there?"

Your loan program should support your goals in owning your home. People waste tens of thousands of dollars because they are in the wrong loan program. The knee-jerk reaction people have is to get the standard 30-year fixed mortgage. Their grandfather had that type of loan, their mom and dad had that type of loan, and therefore they need to have that type of loan. Although the 30-year fixed loan is a great, stable, and predictable loan program, it is not the only loan program out there worth looking into.

Let's get one thing straight. Banks do not sit around and come up with loan programs designed to make the consumer default on the loan. A bank loses money when people go into foreclosure. If a bank's goal was to create such programs, they would be out of business in a short period of time.

As the times change, the housing market changes. What comes along with the housing market changes are new, creative loan programs. So, what are they and which one should you get?

Do you get hit with decisions, decisions, decisions? You will definitely experience that when having to choose the right loan program that harmonizes with your family's future goals.

In this chapter we will identify the most common loan programs. We will answer:

- *What* they are.

- *How* they work.

- *Why* you would choose them.

Here is a general overview of five classifications for the most common programs out on the market today:

1. Conforming fixed loan programs

2. Conforming Adjustable Rate Mortgage (ARM) loan programs

3. Government loan programs

4. Alt – A loan programs

5. Sub-prime loan programs

Note: *We will not identify every loan program out on the market; there are too many to list. You will learn what are the most common and/or popular loan programs consumers are getting today.*

Let's identify what falls under these five classifications for the most common programs:

1. Conforming fixed loan programs

Conforming loan products offer the most aggressive rates. Consumers who are deemed *low-risk* borrowers because of their credit and/or their loan program scenario reap the benefits of such great interest rates. Conforming loans mean loan program's that have guidelines that conform to Fannie Mae or Freddie Mac guidelines. Most people have heard of Fannie Mae and Freddie Mac.

Fannie Mae is short for the Federal National Mortgage Association (FNMA). After the Depression, Fannie Mae was created to bring stability back into the real estate and housing markets. Freddie Mac is short for Federal Home Loan Mortgage Corporation (FHLM). In 1970, Congress chartered a stockholder-owned corporation to purchase and sell residential conventional mortgages. In order for Fannie Mae and Freddie Mac to purchase loans from all major financial institutions, the loans must adhere to their guidelines. They have certain requirements the borrower must meet in order to be able to purchase the loans once they have closed.

What are some of the conforming fixed loan programs?

- 30-year fixed mortgage

- 25-year fixed mortgage

- 20-year fixed mortgage

- 15-year fixed mortgage

- 10-year fixed mortgage

How do these Conforming fixed loan programs work?

These loans are designed to be a fixed-rate mortgage. These loans do not adjust. The first payment at the beginning of the loan will be the same throughout the life of the loan. The only difference between them is the term or length of the loan. The 30-year fixed mortgage is a lower monthly payment than the 15-year mortgage, but the 15-year mortgage will be paid off sooner, i.e., in 15 years, while the 30-year note is amortized or spread over a 30-year period. The longer the term of the loan, the lower the monthly payment. The shorter the term of the loan, the higher the monthly payment.

Why would one want to apply for a conforming fixed loan program?

There are many reasons why you would choose to finance this way. The number one reason is because it is a stable and a predictable way to finance. There is no guesswork on what your mortgage is going to be from one month to the next. Consumers can set their monthly budget around their mortgage payment.

As humans, we love security. A conforming fixed mortgage brings peace of mind knowing today's mortgage payment will be tomorrow's mortgage payment.

Some people's goal is to pay their home off in a certain period of time. Choosing a conforming fixed loan program with a shorter term allows them to achieve their goal. Be strategic when choosing a mortgage program. Your mortgage program very well can be the path that leads you to financial freedom.

2. Conforming Adjustable Rate Mortgage (ARM) loan programs

Conforming loans do not only come in fixed-interest rate programs, but also in Adjustable Rate Mortgages. Sometimes the difference in interest rates between the conforming fixed and the conforming ARM is two to three percent lower. Over the years, Fannie Mae and Freddie Mac have embraced the adjustable rate mortgage market. Their Adjustable Rate Mortgage guidelines now offer clients an "interest only" payment option. ARMs serve a great purpose. As consumers plan the future, they should consider whether an ARM product would be more in line with their goals.

What are some of the Conforming ARM products?

- **1-year ARM**

- **3/1 ARM**

- **5/1 ARM**

- **7/1 ARM**

- **10/1 ARM**

How do these Conforming ARM programs work?

ARM programs adjust. The interest rate changes, typi-cally after a predetermined fixed period. What makes them adjust? The inconsistency of ARM rates is affected directly by the change of index in the market. Every ARM product is tied to a specific index. When the index changes, the interest rate changes, and therefore the mortgage payment adjusts. Here are a few of the indices the ARM programs are tied to (for conforming and non-conforming ARMs):

- **LIBOR (London Interbank Offered Rate)**

- **12 Month MTA or MAT (Monthly Treasury Average)**

- **COSI (Cost Of Savings Index)**

- **CMT or TCM (Constant Maturity Treasury)**

- **COFI (11th District Cost Of Funds)**

- **T-Bill (Treasury Bill)**

- **CD (Certificate of Deposit)**

What seems to be the most frequently used indices are CMT, COFI, COSI and LIBOR.

The conforming ARM programs are great because they

offer a predetermined fixed period before they adjust. The first number before the slash (/) represents the period in which the loan will not adjust. It is considered the fixed period of the loan. The number after the slash (/) represents the adjustment interval. If that number is a "1", that means the loan will adjust annually (*not monthly*). If the number is a "6" (5/6 ARM), it means the loan will adjust every six months (*not years*).

Why would anyone want to apply for a conforming ARM loan program?

There are two popular reasons why someone would want to start off with a conforming ARM loan as opposed to the traditional 30-year fixed.

A. You do not intend to retire in the home and plan on moving within a certain period of time.

If this is you, you need to ask yourself this question: If I know I am only keeping my home for three to five years, why would I want to pay a higher interest rate on a fixed loan program? You could be flushing money down the toilet.

Example: Let's say clients know they are going to move (*for sure*) within three years. At the time of purchase the 30-year fixed interest rate is at 6.5% and the 3/1 ARM (with no prepayment penalty) is at 4.875% (as it was when I bought my home). On a $250,000 loan amount at 6.5% the principle and interest payment equals $1580. The 3/1 ARM at 4.875% principle and interest payment would equal $1323. That is a $257 a month savings.

The 3/1 ARM is more in line with the homeowners' goals and gives them a greater savings. If they got the 30-year fixed because their grandfather had that type of loan, and their mom and dad had that type of loan, then they would have wasted in a 36-month period $9,252.

Most people would look at this scenario and say the 3/1 ARM is the better loan program.

Note: The market changes all the time. Sometimes the interest rates on a 30-year conforming fixed program are just as good as the conforming ARM program. If that is the case, you may want to opt for the conforming fixed product, as your payment difference may be little or none. At least weigh both options before making a decision.

B. You need the lowest monthly payment available. Often the ARM programs offer lower interest rates and therefore a lower monthly payment.

When buying a home, most people are really excited about their potential purchase. They feel as if it is their dream home. They say the same words my wife uttered when we walked through our first home, "I love it!" However, when applying for the loan they found the standard 30-year fixed mortgage payment to be a little beyond their budget. Immediately, the ever-so-common sick feeling in the stomach comes about as they see their ability of owning this wonderful home slip away.

When people find themselves in this position, they will often begin to think about getting an Adjustable Rate

Mortgage. It doesn't matter if they see themselves in their new home for many years.

The ARM program allows their budget to handle such a payment. Plus, never forget, over the next few years there is a great chance your earning potential will increase. After a few raises, you may want to refinance into something more stable if it seems to make sense at the time to do so. The great thing about conforming ARM programs is that they are fixed for a period of a few or more years and typically do not come with a prepayment penalty. In other words, there is no penalty to sell or refinance the loan if needed. ARM programs do give the consumer more buying power.

3. Government loan programs

What are government loans?

There are three types of government loans:

A. **FHA** – Federal Housing Administration

A government agency whose main objective is to under-write residential mortgages loans.

B. **VA** – U.S. Department of Veteran Affairs

A mortgage loan approved by a lending institu-tion to U.S. Veterans that is guaranteed by the Veterans Administration.

C. **RHS** – Rural Housing Services of the U.S. Depart-ment of Agriculture.

Geared to guarantee loans for rural residence by the Rural Housing Services agency.

How do these government loans work?

These loans are supported by government aid. They are insured and guaranteed. This insurance gives assurance to the financier. If the borrower defaults and there is a threat of foreclosure, the financier will have a chance to recoup any potential loss. This makes a mid to high-risk borrower, in many cases, a qualified borrower, simply because of the government backing.

Why would someone want to apply for a government loan?

FHA:

- **Qualifying for a home loan may be easier**. A borrower with lower qualifying features is at times granted approvals because FHA insures their mortgage.

- **Perfect credit is not a necessity.** FHA loans more easily allow borrowers who have had credit problems such as bankruptcy, to qualify for an insured loan.

- **Only minimum down is required.** They will allow as low as 3% down. Whereas most conventional loans will not allow gift funds, FHA does. Your down payment can come as a gift from someone other than you.

- **Costs are lower.** FHA loans have been known to be very competitive with their interest rates. Low interest rates equal low monthly costs.

VA:

- **No money down.** Veterans who would like to purchase a home can do so for no money down. VA loan amounts have exceeded $400,000.

- **No private mortgage insurance.** No mortgage insurance is required, where FHA requires mortgage insurance.

- **Interest rate reduction loan.** Veterans can refinance their current VA loan at little or no expense.

RHS:

- **No required down payment.** The low-to-moderate income families, if qualified, do not need a down payment to purchase a home.

- **Part of the Guaranteed Loan program.** Private sector lenders guarantee the RHS's loans. This means if borrowers default on their loan, the Rural Housing Service will pay the private lender for the loan.

- **Minimal closing costs.** RHS allows qualified homebuyers to acquire loans with minimal closing costs.

These loans are not bad loans, but due to the recent refinance boom, many new conventional loan programs have surfaced. Lending institutions have come out with some aggressive loans that are very competitive with the government loans. Government loans may be your best option. However, do your homework and see if there are other programs that might better suit your needs and pocket-book.

4. Alt-A loan programs

(Not all Alt-A loan programs and scenarios are mentioned in this section)

What are Alt-A loans?

As we discussed in Chapter One, Alt-A loans, also known as "A minus" paper, are where clients possess a strong credit history, but their loan scenario calls for non-traditional underwriting. Alt-A loans are loans that do not conform to the Fannie Mae and/or Freddie Mac guidelines. Alt-A programs are in the middle of "A" paper conforming and sub-prime risk cliental. Alt-A loans offer your basic Fixed and Adjustable Rate Mortgage programs, with and without the interest only monthly payment option.

How do Alt-A loans work?

Because of the non-traditional underwriting guidelines, Alt-A gives clients with strong to decent credit history great loan program alternatives. Some of their guidelines allow for creative documentation concerning clients' income. This helps the strong credit borrower retain a competitive interest rate with a creative/non-traditional loan program.

Here are four common examples of creative Alt-A documentation concerning clients' income: (Refer to the Glossary of Mortgage Terms for further explanation and definitions)

A. Stated Income Stated Assets (SISA) at 100% financing, i.e., less than 5% down (owner occupied).

B. No Income No Assets (NINA) — No mention of income or assets on the loan application.

C. No-Ratio Loan — Debt to income ratios are not a factor.

D. No-Doc Loan — Virtually a signature loan. Great credit is a must!

Why would one want to apply for an Alt-A loan?

Alt-A is a great alternative to the conforming "A" paper loans out on the market. You may have excellent credit but your loan scenario falls outside conforming Fannie Mae/ Freddie Mac guidelines. You may want to do 100% financing on a purchase or refinance. Your debt may be out of control and you need it to not be a factor in qualifying for a home loan, or you may have suddenly joined the ranks of the self-employed (*a No Doc loan may be your best option*). To acquire a loan as a self-employed individual you will have to have had your business for at least two-years. There are many reasons why you may need to go the route of Alt-A, all of which may have nothing to do with you personally, but have to do with the scenario in which you are trying to acquire a loan.

There are banks specific to Alt-A lending, and there are banks that lend not only the conforming "A" paper programs but Alt-A as well. Remember, your credit, your assets, and your work history may be great, but your particular loan scenario, although not bad, may not quite be good enough to conform to traditional guidelines. Alt-A is not a bad way to go in home financing if that is the case.

5. Sub-prime loan programs

The Sub-prime loans are produced by financial institutions and labeled as sub-prime lenders. These lenders' loans serve in such a way to cater to high-risk borrowers. Sub-prime lending is becoming a giant in the mortgage world. They promote zero-down loans, interest-only loans, and even loans for up to 125% of the home's appraised value. Sub-prime lenders offer fixed-rate programs and ARM programs.

What are some Sub-prime loans?

Sub-prime loans are loans that do not conform to the Fannie Mae and/or Freddie Mac guidelines. Here are a few of the common sub-prime loans clients are acquiring:

- **2/28 ARM (may be offered in an interest-only option)**

- **3/27 ARM (may be offered in an interest-only option)**

- **5/25 ARM (may be offered in an interest-only option)**

- **Fixed product (30, 20, and 15 year)**

What do these numbers mean? Just like the conforming ARM programs, the sub-prime ARM's offer a predetermined fixed period before they adjust. The first number before the slash (/) represents the period in which the loan will not adjust. The number after the slash (/) represents how many years the loan will adjust before it is paid in full.

Example: A 2/28 means the loan is fixed for the first two years then will adjust for the remaining 28 years, totaling a 30-year mortgage. The sub-prime market has added a 40-year and some banks even a 50-year amortization period for its ARMs. Instead of a 2/28, which equals 30-years, one may get a lower payment with the 2/38 or 2/48. The 2/38 equals a 40-year note, which in turn offers the client a mortgage payment that is stretched over 40 years (meaning lower monthly payment). These adjustable rate mortgages adjust *monthly* as opposed to the *annual* adjustment the conforming ARM offers after the initial fixed period.

Most of your sub-prime loans *come* with a pre-payment penalty (PPP). They typically come in increments of two years, three years, or five years. A PPP is a penalty charge from the lender to the borrower for paying off a loan prior to an agreed upon (specific) period. This charge may equal up to six months' worth of interest.

Note: *Do not agree to a loan where the PPP **exceeds** the fixed portion of an ARM loan.*

Example: A client has a two-year fixed ARM with a three-year PPP. The loan is fixed for the first two years but will adjust monthly in year three. The client is trapped for year three waiting for the PPP to be up, all the while living with an adjustable rate mortgage that may be going up from month to month.

The sub-prime lender does offer the fixed loan programs, but the majority of their borrowers opt for the adjustable.

Their hope is to improve their credit in a couple of years and then refinance into an "A" paper conforming loan program.

How do these Sub-prime loans work?

These loans are geared more toward the credit-challenged borrower and/or the consumer whose loan is considered a high-risk loan. Sub-prime loans may very well be utilized for the consumer who is considered to be an "A" paper borrower. It is not just the consumer's credit report that dictates the utilization of a sub-prime lender. You may have stellar credit and great assets but want to borrow beyond the actual value of your home. Conforming loans will not support such programs. Two borrowers may have 620 credit scores. One may qualify for conforming, and one may need a sub-prime lender. The compensating factors may differ between the two. One of the borrowers may have a lot of equity, a lot of assets, and great monthly income. The other borrower may need 100% financing, can't qualify with their normal income, and needs to state their income a little higher on their application without having to prove it (Stated Income Loan). They also have no assets, and they are trying to refinance their home that was just taken off the market and listed with Multiple Listing Services (MLS, i.e., find homes, properties, and houses listed in the market). Two borrowers, the same credit scores but two totally different loan risks. Therefore, the one borrower may need a sub-prime lender who specializes in dealing with high-risk loan scenarios and high-risk borrowers.

How are these lenders able to qualify a borrower when conforming loans deny them? The answer: the sub-prime lender's investor. All sub-prime lenders have their set of investors they will sell the loan to once the loan has been funded. These various investors have their own set of guidelines. The sub-prime lenders need to adhere to their investor's loan program guidelines. If they do not, the investor will not buy the loan from the sub-prime company who originated it.

The investor guidelines are more lenient than the conforming guidelines. They may allow the clients debt-to-income (DTI) ratio (*a measure that compares people's debt payments to their gross monthly income*) to be as high as 55% but may have stipulations in the guidelines that allow for exceptions up to a 60% DTI. Conforming guidelines prefer their clients to be at a 45% DTI. If clients go beyond 45%, they must have other compensating factors that still make them strong borrowers.

What comes with lenient guidelines are higher interest rates with prepayment penalties. These investors are dealing with high-risk loans/borrowers. Higher interest rates and pre-payment penalties are there for the investors' return on a high-risk investment. Since the investors know their clients are high-risk, they run the risk of their cliental defaulting on their mortgage payment. High-risk clients get higher interest rates (*most of the time*).

Why would one want to apply for a Sub-prime loan?

When clients cannot qualify for the conforming "A" paper or non-conforming Alt-A loan programs, the sub-prime lender may be their initial answer to getting into a home. Yes, they may pay a higher interest rate but still qualify financially for a home. It is still better to pay a higher interest rate on a home than no interest rate on a rental.

A very popular sub-prime loan is the 2/28. The 2/28 may be the entry-level program borrowers with poor credit need to help achieve their goal. Borrowers will usually not stay in this loan program. They will take advantage of the first two years fixed portion of the loan to clean up their credit. When the two years are up, they plan to refinance into a conforming loan program, possibly a fixed-rate mortgage. They use the 2/28-loan program as a stepping-stone in the right direction.

Before choosing a loan program, identify your goals concerning your home. Once you know where you want to go, you can choose the loan program that will best take you there.

Note: Loan programs are volatile in nature and subject to change. Examples in this chapter are for reference only. All consumers should consult with their local mortgage professional for the most recent rates and underwriting guidelines.

9

Paperwork, Paperwork, Paperwork

What are these Forms and what do they Mean?

The papers you will come in contact with are as confusing as they are numerous. You can read page after page and still may not understand what it is you are reading. If you find yourself dealing with that, rest assured, you are normal!

f you are like most people, you are not a fan of paperwork. If you think about it, paperwork has been part of our lives ever since the day we were born. When we were born, our parents had to fill out the necessary paperwork. When we started school, more paperwork was needed for the school district (shot records, etc.). Going to school caused an enormous amount of paperwork through this most popular avenue: *homework*. Applying for college or a job required paperwork. When getting married, we fill out paperwork for the license. When purchasing a car, there are various forms of paperwork that are needed. Applying for a loan of any size requires paperwork. Even when we die, family members are stuck with . . . paperwork.

How about when purchasing or refinancing a home? That is an emphatic, YES! When purchasing a home, you will eventually fill out the mother-load of all paperwork. At signing you will literally feel as if you are signing a phone book, especially if you are acquiring a first and a second mortgage.

The papers you will come in contact with are as confusing as they are numerous. You can read page after page and still may not understand what it is that you are reading. If you find yourself dealing with that, rest assured you are normal.

When I view the loan process in its entirety, I have experienced clients receiving up to three sets of paperwork.

1. The initial set of disclosures sent from the loan agent.

2. A set of forms from the actual bank that will be financing the borrower's loan.

3. The final paperwork to be signed at the closing of the loan.

What are all of these disclosure forms about? Let's look at the initial set of forms clients should receive from their loan agent and/or mortgage company. Know that different mortgage companies may send additional forms. If you are going directly through a bank, they only have to send certain types of forms. If you are using a mortgage broker, additional forms (comparative to the bank forms) may be required for you to sign. Some banks the mortgage broker utilizes may require the client to sign additional forms specific to their bank, per their investors. If you compare all the forms various loan agents send their clients, there are a select few that are generic enough to apply to most lending.

Let's identify some of these generic forms most clients will get early on in the loan process. The sample disclosure forms you will see are from the bank PMAC Lending Services. PMAC Lending Services is out of Chino Hills, California. Compliance is one of their core values. These sample forms (disclosures) are what their loan agents send out to their prospective clients.

Note: *The disclosures the client receives may be tuned to the look and feel of the bank they are acquiring the loan from, as well as differing due to the mortgage software the loan agent may be using. Although the look of the disclosures may differ between banks the content is the same.*

CREDIT INFORMATION AUTHORIZATION

TO WHOM IT MAY CONCERN:
The undersigned applicant has applied for a real estate loan with PMAC Lending Services, Inc. The applicant(s) signature below authorizes you to release the information requested on the attached form.

I HEREBY AUTHORIZE YOU TO RELEASE ANY INFORMATION REQUIRED BY PMAC LENDING SERVICES, INC. OR ITS ASSIGNS IN CONNECTION WITH THE ABOVE REFERENCED LOAN, EITHER BEFORE THE LOAN IS CLOSED OR AS PART OF ITS QUALITY ASSURANCE PROGRAM. NECESSARY CREDIT INFORMATION MAY INCLUDE, BUT IS NOT LIMITED TO: A CONSUMER CREDIT REPORT, EMPLOYMENT HISTORY AND INCOME, SAVINGS DEPOSIT(S), CHECKING ACCOUNT(S), CONSUMER CREDIT BALANCES, PAYMENTS AND HISTORY AND COPIES OF INCOME TAX RETURNS.

SIGN HERE

Borrower Signature   Date

SIGN HERE

Co-Borrower Signature   Date

PHOTOCOPIES OF THIS AUTHORIZATION ARE TO BE ACCEPTED AS THE ORIGINAL.

Privacy Act Notice: This information is to be used by the agency collecting it in determining whether you qualify as a prospective mortgagor under its program. It will not be disclosed outside the agency without your consent except to your employer(s) for verification of employment and as required and permitted by law. The information requested on the attached form is authorized by Title 38, U.S.C., Chapter 37 (If VA), by 12 U.S.C., Section 1701 et. seq. (IF HUD/FHA) and Title 42 U.S.C., 1471 et. seq. or 1921 et. seq. (If U.S.D.A. FmHA).

Notice to Borrower(s): This serves as notice to you, as required by the Right to Financial Privacy Act of 1978, that HUD/FHA has a right of access to financial records held by financial institutions in connection with the consideration or administration of assistance to you. Financial records involving your transaction will be available to HUD/FHA without further notice or authorization but will not be disclosed or released by this institution to another Government Agency or Department without your consent except as required or permitted by law.

Notice to Borrower(s): Appraisal and credit report fees are required upon application of the loan. These fees are incurred on your behalf through outside sources and are non-refundable regardless of whether the loan is approved, canceled, or declined.

©2005 PMAC Lending Services, Inc
CONFIDENTIAL

Conventional Loan Application Kit
Page 2 of 8

This form gives the mortgage company authorization to run the clients' credit and release any required information about their credit to the bank that is financing the loan.

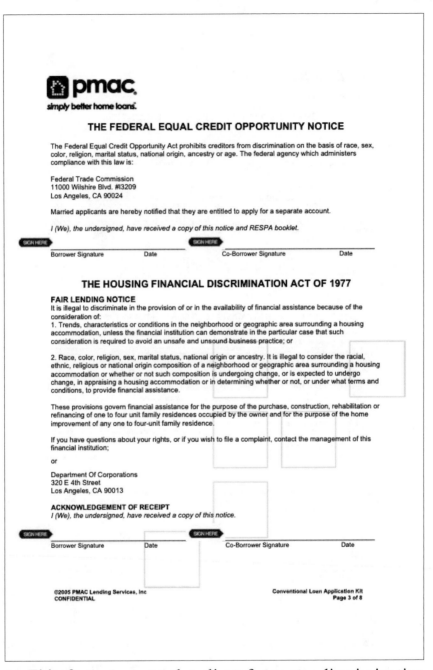

This form protects the client from any discrimination from a lender on the basis of race, sex, color, religion, etc.

pmac.
simply better home loans.

NOTICE REGARDING APPRAISAL REPORT

RE:_____
      PROPERTY ADDRESS   CITY   ST   ZIP

You have the right to a copy of the appraisal report to be obtained in connection with the loan for which you are applying, provided that you have paid for the appraisal. This notice is not a request for a copy of the appraisal report. It is only to advise you of how you may obtain a copy of this report. If you want a copy of the appraisal, please submit a separate written request no later than 90 days after a decision has been made on your loan request. Please address your request to:

PMAC Lending Services, Inc.
100 N. CITRUS STREET SUITE #430
WEST COVINA , CA 91791
ATTN: QUALITY ASSURANCE

I (we) fully understand that the sole purpose of the appraisal is to assist PMAC Lending Services, Inc. in evaluating the property for lending purposes only. The appraisal was not and is not intended for the use of a loan applicant and should not be relied upon for such purpose, as neither the appraiser nor PMAC warrants the value or the condition of the property for any other parties.

I (we) further understand and agree that the appraisal, or any part of the appraisal, including the conclusion as to the property value, cannot be used by any but PMAC Lending Services, Inc. or its successors, assigns and mortgage insurers.

I (we) agree not to hold PMAC Lending Services, Inc. liable, now or in the future, for the appraisal report, including but not limited to: estimates, opinions, conditions and value.

The signature(s) below acknowledges your receipt of a copy of this notice of your right to a copy of the appraisal report.

SIGN HERE
_____   _____
Borrower   Date

_____   _____
Address   City   State   Zip

SIGN HERE
_____   _____
Co-Borrower   Date

_____   _____
Address   City   State   Zip

©2005 PMAC Lending Services, Inc   Conventional Loan Application Kit
CONFIDENTIAL   Page 4 of 8

This form is letting clients know they have a right to the appraisal report in connection with the property they are financing.

Note: **ONLY** if the client has paid for the appraisal.

SERVICING DISCLOSURE STATEMENT

<u>NOTICE TO FIRST LIEN MORTGAGE LOAN APPLICANTS:</u> THE RIGHT TO COLLECT YOUR MORTGAGE LOAN PAYMENTS MAY BE TRANSFERRED. FEDERAL LAW GIVES YOU CERTAIN RELATED RIGHTS. IF YOUR LOAN IS MADE, SAVE THIS STATEMENT WITH YOUR LOAN DOCUMENTS. READ THIS STATEMENT AND SIGN IT ONLY IF YOU UNDERSTAND ITS CONTENTS.

Because you are applying for a mortgage loan covered by the Real Estate Settlement Procedures Act (RESPA) (12 U.S.C. §2601 et seq.) you have certain rights under that federal law. This statement tells you about those rights. It also tells you what the chances are that the servicing for this loan may be transferred to a different loan servicer.

"Servicing" refers to collecting your principal, interest and escrow account payments, if any. If your loan servicer changes, there are certain procedures that must be followed. This statement generally explains those procedures.

TRANSFER PRACTICES AND REQUIREMENTS

If the servicing of your loan is assigned, sold, or transferred to a new servicer, you must be given written notice of that transfer. The present loan servicer must send you notice in writing of the assignment, sale or transfer of the servicing not less than 15 days before the date of the transfer. The new loan servicer must also send you notice within 15 days after the date of the transfer. The present servicer and the new servicer may combine this information in one notice so long as the notice is sent to you 15 days before the effective date of transfer. The 15 day period is not applicable if a notice of prospective transfer is provided to you at settlement. The law allows a delay in the time (not more than 30 days after a transfer) for servicers to notify upon the occurrence of certain business emergencies.

The notices must contain certain information. They must contain the effective date of the transfer of the servicing of your loan to the new servicer, the name, address, and toll-free or collect-call telephone numbers of the new servicer, and toll-free or collect-call telephone numbers of a person or department for both your present servicer and your new servicer to answer your questions. During the 60-day period following the effective date of the transfer of the loan servicing, a loan payment received by your old servicer before its due date may not be treated by the new loan servicer as late, and a late fee may not be imposed on you.

COMPLAINT RESOLUTION

Section 6 of RESPA (12 U.S.C. §2605) gives you certain consumer rights, whether or not your loan servicing is transferred. If you send a "qualified written request to your loan servicer, your servicer must provide you with a written acknowledgment within 20 business days of receipt of your request. A "qualified written request" is a written correspondence, other than notice on a payment coupon or other payment medium supplied by the servicer, which includes your name and account number, and your reasons for the request. Not later than 60 business days after receiving your request, your servicer must make any appropriate corrections to your account or must provide you with a written clarification regarding any dispute. During this 60 day period, your servicer may not provide information to a consumer reporting agency concerning any overdue payment related to such period or qualified written request.

A business day is any day in which the offices of the business entity are open to the public for carrying on substantially all of its business functions.

DAMAGES AND COSTS

Section 6 of RESPA also provides for damages and costs for individuals or classes of individuals in circumstances where servicers are shown to have violated the requirements of that section.

Conventional Loan Application Kit
Page 5 of 8

This is typically page 1 of 2 of the servicing disclosure. This page explains that the servicing (who's collecting the mortgage payments) function of the client's loan may be transferred. This form explains the general procedures banks must adhere to when transferring between servicers takes place.

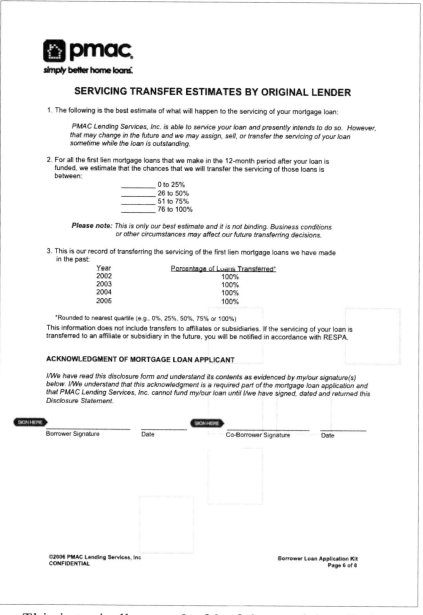

pmac
simply better home loans.

SERVICING TRANSFER ESTIMATES BY ORIGINAL LENDER

1. The following is the best estimate of what will happen to the servicing of your mortgage loan:

   PMAC Lending Services, Inc. is able to service your loan and presently intends to do so. However, that may change in the future and we may assign, sell, or transfer the servicing of your loan sometime while the loan is outstanding.

2. For all the first lien mortgage loans that we make in the 12-month period after your loan is funded, we estimate that the chances that we will transfer the servicing of those loans is between:

   _____ 0 to 25%
   _____ 26 to 50%
   _____ 51 to 75%
   _____ 76 to 100%

   Please note: This is only our best estimate and it is not binding. Business conditions or other circumstances may affect our future transferring decisions.

3. This is our record of transferring the servicing of the first lien mortgage loans we have made in the past:

Year	Percentage of Loans Transferred*
2002	100%
2003	100%
2004	100%
2005	100%

*Rounded to nearest quartile (e.g., 0%, 25%, 50%, 75% or 100%)

This information does not include transfers to affiliates or subsidiaries. If the servicing of your loan is transferred to an affiliate or subsidiary in the future, you will be notified in accordance with RESPA.

ACKNOWLEDGMENT OF MORTGAGE LOAN APPLICANT

I/We have read this disclosure form and understand its contents as evidenced by my/our signature(s) below. I/We understand that this acknowledgment is a required part of the mortgage loan application and that PMAC Lending Services, Inc. cannot fund my/our loan until I/we have signed, dated and returned this Disclosure Statement.

SIGN HERE _____   SIGN HERE _____
Borrower Signature   Date   Co-Borrower Signature   Date

©2006 PMAC Lending Services, Inc
CONFIDENTIAL

Borrower Loan Application Kit
Page 6 of 8

This is typically page 2 of 2 of the servicing disclosure. This form explains what percentages of loans in the past have been sold and/or transferred. This communicates the future possibility of such action taking place concerning the servicing of the clients' loan.

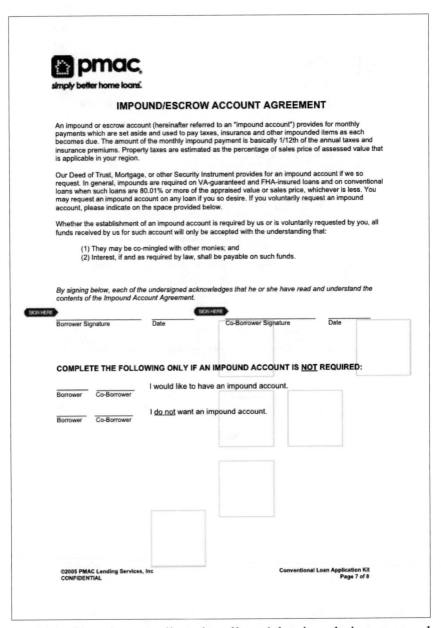

This form is regarding the clients' having their taxes and insurance in the mortgage payment. Regardless if the clients choose to have their taxes and insurance in the mortgage payment, this form explains the nature of establishing such a process, as well as the lenders' rights in dealing with such funds.

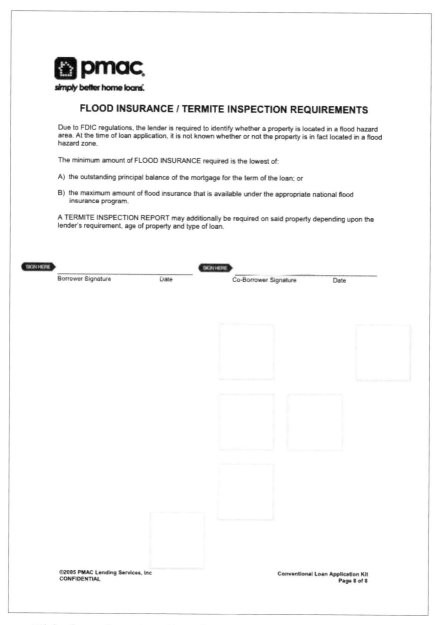

This form lets the client know that the lender will need to confirm whether the subject property is or is not in a flood zone. Also, it communicates that a termite inspection may be required when more information on the property is known.

The second set of paperwork sent to the client has a lot to do with banks' being RESPA compliant. RESPA is the Real Estate Settlement Procedures Act, a Federal consumer protection statute first enacted in 1974. This Act protects the borrower by making the lenders disclose certain documents that reveal the reality of what they are getting in the way of a loan program, as well as what they are being charged. There are two forms the clients must receive within 72 hours of submitting their loan application:

1. Good Faith Estimate (*definition in glossary of terms*)

2. Truth-in-Lending Statement (*definition in glossary of terms*)

Here are samples of what the Good Faith Estimate and the Truth-in-Lending disclosure form may look like:

Note: *These forms may differ in appearance between banks, as they may be tuned to the their particular look and feel, as well as differing due to the mortgage software the loan agent may be utilizing. However, the content communicates the same.*

pmac.
simply better home loans.

Borrower Cost Estimate

Mortgage Type: Refinance

Borrower Information

Borrower(s) Name	John Doe
Street Address	1111 Address Lane
City, State, ZIP	Federal Way, WA 98003
eMail Address	
Phone #	0
Referring Agent	0
Office Address	0
eMail	0
Fax #	0

Subject Property

Street Address	1111 Address Lane
City, State, ZIP	Federal Way, WA 98003
	Single Family
Type	Home

Subject Property Mortgage Information

Value of Home	$	380,000.00
Loan Payoff	$	261,782.00
Current Loan Interest Rate		Enter Current Rate
New Loan Amount	$	304,000.00
Loan to Value (LTV)		80.00%
Target Rate		6.000%
Amortization Term In Months		360
Loan Type		Fixed
Loan Origination Points		1.000%
Loan Discount Points		0.000%
PrePay Years		
Escrow Impounds		Yes
Interest Only Option		FALSE
Your Fico Score		720

Monthly Payment Analysis

1st Mortgage Principal & Interest (P&I)	$	1,822.63
Monthly Taxes	$	356.25
Hazard Insurance	$	48.95
Interest Only Payment Option	$	-

Your Total Monthly Payments (3)	**$**	**2,227.83**
Interest Only Option		

Total Closing Costs

New Loan Amount	$	304,000.00
Old Loan Payoff	$	261,782.00
Borrower Prepaid Expenses	$	3,191.20
Total Lending Costs	$	6,020.00
Credit Given by Seller	$	-
Credit Given by Lender	$	-

Cash (From) / To You At Closing (1)	**$**	**33,006.80**

Breakdown of Your Lending Fees

PMAC Loan Costs	$	4,035.00
Third Party Fees	$	1,985.00
Appraisal & Credit	$	450.00
Loan Origination	$	3,040.00
Loan Discount	$	-
Processing	$	300.00
Underwriting	$	300.00
Documentation	$	235.00
Wire Transfer	$	50.00
FEMA	$	45.00
Tax Service	$	65.00
Escrow Services (Third Party)	$	550.00
Title Insurance (Third Party)	$	950.00
Recording	$	35.00
PAD (Third Party) (4)	$	150.00

Borrower Pre Paid Expenses	$	3,191.20
Property Taxes if Due (2)	$	2,137.50
6 Months Homeowners Insurance	$	293.70
15 Days of Interest on New Loan (2)	$	760.00

Notes:

1 - All fees are estimated and based on initial credit information, current rates, and the appraised value. Rates
2 - All property taxes and homeowners insurance must be paid current at or through closing. Homeowners
3 - Your total monthly payments do not include provisions for taxes and insurance which may be required.
4 - PMAC includes a PAD to act as a cushion for any unplanned fees relative to third party fees. All unused

Loan Agent's Name
Loan Officer, PMAC

For more information, please contact me at:
Phone # 800-710-PMAC
eMail Loan Agent's email address

PMAC Lending Services
Good Faith Estimate

TRUTH-IN-LENDING DISCLOSURE STATEMENT
(THIS IS NEITHER A CONTRACT NOR A COMMITMENT TO LEND)

Applicants:

Property Address:

Application No:

Prepared By: **PMAC LENDING SERVICES, INC.**
15325 FAIRFIELD RANCH ROAD, #200
CHINO HILLS , CA 91709
909-614-2000

Date Prepared:

ANNUAL PERCENTAGE RATE	FINANCE CHARGE	AMOUNT FINANCED	TOTAL OF PAYMENTS
The cost of your credit as a yearly rate	The dollar amount the credit will cost you	The amount of credit provided to you or on your behalf	The amount you will have paid after making all payments as scheduled
* 7.500 %	$ * 579,080.23	$ * 379,690.32	$ * 958,770.55

REQUIRED DEPOSIT: The annual percentage rate does not take into account your required deposit
PAYMENTS: Your payment schedule will be:

Number of Payments	Amount of Payments **	When Payments Are Due	Number of Payments	Amount of Payments **	When Payments Are Due	Number of Payments	Amount of Payments **	When Payments Are Due
		Monthly Beginning:			Monthly Beginning:			Monthly Beginning:
359	2,663.24							
1	2,667.39							

DEMAND FEATURE: This obligation has a demand feature.
VARIABLE RATE FEATURE: This loan contains a variable rate feature. A variable rate disclosure has been provided earlier.

CREDIT LIFE/CREDIT DISABILITY: Credit life insurance and credit disability insurance are not required to obtain credit, and will not be provided unless you sign and agree to pay the additional cost.

Type	Premium	Signature
Credit Life		I want credit life insurance. Signature:
Credit Disability		I want credit disability insurance. Signature:
Credit Life and Disability		I want credit life and disability insurance. Signature:

INSURANCE: The following insurance is required to obtain credit:
☐ Credit life insurance ☐ Credit disability ☑ Property insurance ☐ Flood insurance
You may obtain the insurance from anyone you want that is acceptable to creditor
☑ If you purchase ☑ property ☐ flood insurance from creditor you will pay $ for a one year term.
SECURITY: You are giving a security interest in:
☑ The goods or property being purchased ☐ Real property you already own.
FILING FEES: $
LATE CHARGE: If a payment is more than **15** days late, you will be charged **5.000** % of the payment
PREPAYMENT: If you pay off early, you
☐ may ☑ will not have to pay a penalty.
☐ may ☑ will not be entitled to a refund of part of the finance charge.
ASSUMPTION: Someone buying your property
☐ may ☐ may, subject to conditions ☑ may not assume the remainder of your loan on the original terms.
See your contract documents for any additional information about nonpayment, default, any required repayment in full before the scheduled date and prepayment refunds and penalties.
☑ * means an estimate ☑ all dates and numerical disclosures except the late payment disclosures are estimates.
* * NOTE: The Payments shown above include reserve deposits for Mortgage Insurance (if applicable), but exclude Property Taxes and Insurance.

THE UNDERSIGNED ACKNOWLEDGES RECEIVING A COMPLETED COPY OF THIS DISCLOSURE.

_____ (Applicant) (Date)   _____ (Applicant) (Date)

_____ (Applicant) (Date)   _____ (Applicant) (Date)

_____ (Lender) (Date)

TRUTH-IN-LENDING DISCLOSURE STATEMENT

The most paperwork a client will deal with will come at the end of the loan process. In order to secure the loan, the client will need to do a final signing. We are unable to give samples of each page as the volume of papers is too great.

After the escrow agent works up the final paperwork, the loan agent should request to see a particular document. This document is referred to as the HUD, HUD1, or Settlement Statement. This document communicates all the costs of the loan. It will reveal what the client will bring in at closing or get back at closing. It is a good idea for the loan agents to review such a document to make sure there are no clerical errors. Once they have reviewed the Settlement Statement and feel comfortable, they can do what I term as a "Post Close." This is a final review of the loan program and cost with the client before the signing. The loan agents will go over the Settlement Statement with the client. This way the clients know what the actual costs are coming to. This is also comforting as they will already know what they are going to see at signing before the actually see it. Doing the "Post Close" makes for a smooth signing.

Here is a sample of the Settlement Statement borrowers will see at time of signing:

A. Settlement Statement

U.S. Department of Housing and Urban Development

OMB Approval No. 2502-0265

B. Type of Loan

1. ☐ FHA	2. ☐ FmHA	3. ☐ Conv. Unins.	6. File Number: 9999999	7. Loan Number: 9999999	8. Mortgage Insurance Case Number: 99-99-9-9999999
4. ☑ VA	5. ☐ Conv. Ins.				

C. Note: This form is furnished to give you a statement of actual settlement costs. Amounts paid to and by the settlement agent are shown. Items marked "(p.o.c.)" were paid outside the closing; they are shown here for informational purposes and are not included in the totals.

D. Name & Address of Borrower:	E. Name & Address of Seller:	F. Name & Address of Lender:
John Q. DOE Mary Q. DOE 98 Washington Street Anytown, US 99999	Timothy A. SMITH 76 Elm Street Anytown, US 99999	ANYTOWN BANK 123 Main Street Anytown, US 99999

G. Property Location:	H. Settlement Agent:
98 Washington Street Anytown, US 99999 Lot 1, Bl. 23, Sec. 45 N. Anytown Washington County, US	Anytown Settlement Agency
	Place of Settlement: 987 Main Street Suite 100 Anytown, US 99999
	I. Settlement Date: 06/29/2003

J. Summary of Borrower's Transaction		K. Summary of Seller's Transaction	
100. Gross Amount Due From Borrower		**400. Gross Amount Due To Seller**	
101. Contract sales price	196,000.00	401. Contract sales price	196,000.00
102. Personal property		402. Personal property	
103. Settlement charges to borrower (line 1400)	4,540.74	403.	
104.		404.	
105.		405.	
Adjustments for items paid by seller in advance		**Adjustments for items paid by seller in advance**	
106. City/town taxes to		406. City/town taxes to	
107. County taxes 6/29 to 6/30	11.31	407. County taxes 6/29 to 6/30	11.31
108. Assessments to		408. Assessments to	
109.		409.	
110.		410.	
111.		411.	
112.		412.	
120. Gross Amount Due From Borrower	200,552.05	**420. Gross Amount Due To Seller**	196,011.31
200. Amounts Paid By Or In Behalf Of Borrower		**500. Reductions In Amount Due To Seller**	
201. Deposit or earnest money	1,000.00	501. Excess deposit (see instructions)	
202. Principal amount of new loan(s)	196,000.00	502. Settlement charges to seller (line 1400)	10,474.00
203. Existing loan(s) taken subject to		503. Existing loan(s) taken subject to	
204.		504. Payoff of first mortgage loan	105,297.12
205.		505. Payoff of second mortgage loan	
206.		506. Payoff Processing/Delivery	25.00
207.		507. Home Warranty	325.00
208.		508. Rent Back Security Deposit	1,000.00
209. Rent Back 6/29 to 7/10 @ 49.95	649.35	509. Rent Back 6/29 to 7/10 @ 49.95	649.35
Adjustments for items unpaid by seller		**Adjustments for items unpaid by seller**	
210. City/town taxes to		510. City/town taxes to	
211. County taxes to		511. County taxes to	
212. Assessments to		512. Assessments to	
213.		513. 1st 1/2 1998 RE Taxes #999-9-99-99-999	1,023.82
214.		514.	
215.		515.	
216.		516.	
217.		517.	
218.		518.	
219.		519.	
220. Total Paid By/For Borrower	197,649.35	**520. Total Reduction Amount Due Seller**	118,794.29
300. Cash At Settlement From/To Borrower		**600. Cash At Settlement To/From Seller**	
301. Gross Amount due from borrower (line 120)	200,552.05	601. Gross amount due to seller (line 420)	196,011.31
302. Less amounts paid by/for borrower (line 200)	(197,649.35)	602. Less reductions in amt. due seller (line 520)	(118,794.29)
303. Cash ☑ From ☐ To Borrower	2,902.70	**603. Cash** ☑ To ☐ From Seller	77,217.02

Section 5 of the Real Estate Settlement Procedures Act (RESPA) requires the following: • HUD must develop a Special Information Booklet to help persons borrowing money to finance the purchase of residential real estate to better understand the nature and costs of real estate settlement services; • Each lender must provide the booklet to all applicants from whom it receives or for whom it prepares a written application to borrow money to finance the purchase of residential real estate; • Lenders must prepare and distribute with the Booklet a Good Faith Estimate of the settlement costs that the borrower is likely to incur in connection with the settlement. These disclosures are mandatory.

Section 4(a) of RESPA mandates that HUD develop and prescribe this standard form to be used at the time of loan settlement to provide full disclosure of all charges imposed upon the borrower and seller. These are third party disclosures that are designed to provide the borrower with pertinent information during the settlement process in order to be a better shopper.

The Public Reporting Burden for this collection of information is estimated to average one hour per response, including the time for reviewing instructions, searching existing data sources, gathering and maintaining the data needed, and completing and reviewing the collection of information.

This agency may not collect this information, and you are not required to complete this form, unless it displays a currently valid OMB control number. The information requested does not lend itself to confidentiality.

Previous editions are obsolete

Page 1 of 2

form HUD-1 (3/86) ref Handbook 4305.2

HUD, ESTIMATED HUD OR SETTLEMENT STATEMENT – Page 1 of 2

L. Settlement Charges

700. Total Sales/Broker's Commission based on price $ 196,000.00 @ 5.00 % = 9,800.00		Paid From Borrowers Funds at Settlement	Paid From Seller's Funds at Settlement
Division of Commission (line 700) as follows:			
701. $ 5,880.00 to Anytown Real Estate			
702. $ 3,920.00 to Anytown Properties			
703. Commission paid at Settlement			9,800
704. Deposit held by Anytown Real Estate	$1000		
800. Items Payable In Connection With Loan			
801. Loan Origination Fee 1 % ANYTOWN BANK		1,960.00	
802. Loan Discount %			
803. Appraisal Fee to James Jones 300B			
804. Credit Report to ABC Credit Reports 58B			
805. Lender's Inspection Fee			
806. Mortgage Insurance Application Fee to			
807. Assumption Fee			
808. Tax Service Contract ANYTOWN BANK		65.00	
809. Flood Cert. Fee ANYTOWN BANK		21.50	
810.			
811.			
900. Items Required By Lender To Be Paid In Advance			
901. Interest from 06/29/98 to 07/01/98 @$ 37.59 /day		75.18	
902. Mortgage Insurance Premium for months to			
903. Hazard Insurance Premium for years to			
904. years to			
905.			
1000. Reserves Deposited With Lender			
1001. Hazard insurance 2 months @$ 24.15 per month		48.30	
1002. Mortgage insurance months @$ per month			
1003. City property taxes months @$ per month			
1004. County property taxes 2 months @$ 170.64 per month		341.28	
1005. Annual assessments months @$ per month			
1006. months @$ per month			
1007. months @$ per			
1008. Aggregate Adjustment		-144.92	
1100. Title Charges			
1101. Settlement or closing fee to Anytown Settlement Agency			195.00
1102. Abstract or title search to			
1103. Title examination to ABCIC		243.00	
1104. Title insurance binder to			
1105. Document preparation to Watson & Watson, PLC			125.00
1106. Notary fees to			
1107. Attorney's fees to			
(includes above item numbers:)			
1108. Title insurance to Anytown Land Title Insurance Company		831.40	
(includes above items numbers: 1104 & ALTA 8.1)			
1109. Lender's coverage $ 196,000.00 — 585.40			
1110. Owner's coverage $ 196,000.00 — 246.00			
1111. RS-E Filing Fee Anytown Settlement Agency			25.00
1112. Release Processing Anytown Settlement Agency			85.00
1113.			
1200. Government Recording and Transfer Charges			
1201. Recording fees: Deed $ 17.00 : Mortgage $ 16.00 : Releases $ 16.00		33.00	16.00
1202. City/county tax/stamps: Deed $ 98.00 : Mortgage $ 98.00		196.00	
1203. State tax/stamps: Deed $ 294.00 : Mortgage $ 294.00		588.00	
1204. Grantors Tax			196.00
1205. Record Assignment		16.00	
1300. Additional Settlement Charges			
1301. Survey to Andrew V. Johnson		235.00	
1302. Pest inspection to			
1303. Record POA and Affidavit Clerk of Court		32.00	32.00
1304.			
1305.			
1400. Total Settlement Charges (enter on lines 103, Section J and 502, Section K)		4,540.74	10,474.00

Previous editions are obsolete   Page 2 of 2   form **HUD-1** (3/86)
                                                             ref Handbook 4305.2

HUD, ESTIMATED HUD OR SETTLEMENT STATEMENT – Page 2 of 2

Paperwork, paperwork, paperwork! It will be part of our lives until the end. As a client, if you do not understand what it is that you are asked to sign, simply do not sign it. Do not be forced into anything. If you feel that you are being rushed at the signing table, let them know you have the right to understand what it is you are signing.

The purpose of your loan will determine if you have a three-day right of rescission, which simply means that after the clients sign, they have three days to change their mind and cancel the loan. If you do not have all day at the signing table, which most people do not, you can always request a set of the documents you signed, especially if the three-day right of rescission applies to you. A lot of borrowers will go home and review the documents. If something is wrong, they can contact their loan agent to try to rectify the perceived error. If the error cannot be rectified, they can simply cancel the loan if they would like.

You will not become an expert in understanding all the documents you sign through the loan process. However, you can be an informed borrower and understand the gist of what it is you are signing.

Do not let the paperwork of the loan process overwhelm you. It is normal, and your loan agent is there to help you understand it.

Chapter

10

The Loan Process Playbook
Get Informed — Get in Control — Get in the Loop

*When acquiring a loan you are joining a team.
You are part of a team of people whose goal is to
fund your loan. You are suddenly part of the mortgage
financing game. The end result is a wonderful trophy:
your home!*

F or the first time at the age of 10, I played tackle football. I played touch football with friends during recess at school, but this was the first time I would be putting on the helmet and pads and actually learning the game.

I remember my first practice. I had no idea what to expect. The first week was all about conditioning. We ran and ran and ran at every practice. Peppered throughout our running, the coaches would teach the fundamentals of the game. They began to describe all the different positions. They explained what they were, where and when they would be on the football field, and what type of individual would work best at which position.

If you were a fast runner, you may be considered for a running back position or wide receiver. If you had a good arm and you could throw a football with accuracy, you might be looked at as a quarterback. If you were one of the bigger kids on the team and were considered strong, you might fit well as a lineman. I was quick for my age so my coach positioned me as a wide receiver.

My coach gave every player on the team a playbook consisting of many different plays we would run in a game. It did not matter what position you were in, we each had to learn all the plays we might run in the games we'd play. For me this meant, I had to be familiar with what the other positions/players were doing on each play, but I did not have to memorize each position's plays. However, I did have to be familiar with what all the players were going to be doing in each play. Familiarizing myself with all the positions and their assignments gave me a better understanding of how we as a team would work as a unit and how my role/position would fit within the unit.

Within a short period of time, I understood more clearly the role I played on our football team, the positions other players played, and most important, who had what responsibilities at what time during the game. Our team had eleven young boys out on the field, all playing different positions, all having different responsibilities, but all playing together and working toward a common goal . . . to WIN!

The loan process for your mortgage is very similar. You are part of a team of people whose goal is to fund your loan. You are suddenly part of the mortgage financing *game*. The end result is a wonderful trophy: your home!

You want to win this mortgage financing game. You want to be the victor. It is the hardworking culmination of a team that can make your desire of winning this game a reality. Vince Lombardi puts it best, "Individual commitment to a **group effort - that is** what makes a team work, a company work, a society work, a civilization work."

There are many different people working on your transaction. Many people feel it is just their loan agent who works on their file because that is whom they interact with most. It is quite the contrary. Your loan agent is one of many different people working on your loan.

In this chapter you will discover:

- Who is on your team along with their responsibilities.

- The length of the game (the loan process time frame).

- How the game is played (the order in which you play).

- Your position and what is expected of you.

The process I will walk you through is going to be the basics of what you will experience. Banks may differ a little in the function of closing your loan. For the most part, the loan process is generic enough to cross over from bank to bank.

The understanding you will gain from this chapter will make you feel informed, in control, and in the loop.

Let's first identify who is on your team. Who is your starting line-up, the *major* players, and what are their responsibilities?

Note: *This list is not all-inclusive as there may be other contributors supporting the major players and different banks may title positions differently.*

WHO IS ON MY TEAM?

Loan Agent: An employee of a lending institution who originates loans for their company. Often referred to as Loan Officer, Mortgage Banker, Account Executive, etc. Loan agents will often counsel and direct the borrower to the appropriate loan program.

Real Estate Agent(s): One who acts for or represents the buyer or seller in a real estate sales transaction.

Loan Processor: One who handles the borrowers' file by organizing their information and makes sure everything is ready for Underwriting.

Underwriter: The people who approve or deny mortgage loans by following mortgage standards and guidelines. They review and evaluate information on mortgage loan documents to determine if buyer, property, and loan conditions meet establishment and/or government standards.

Doc Drawer: A department within the lending institution that draws (prepares) the final documentation (docs) the borrower signs at the closing of the loan. They prepare the docs, along with any instructions from the lender to the escrow company. They then forward them by email or overnight delivery to Escrow.

Funder: One who does the final checks and balances on the loan after the borrower has signed the final paperwork. Once all the lenders' conditions are met/satisfied, they will release the funds to close the borrowers' loan.

Appraiser: A qualified individual who through education, training, and experience provides a written report that estimates a property's current market value.

Title Company: A company that provides title insurance. Their insurance protects the lender and/or owner against loss in the event of property ownership disputes.

The title company has a representative who will be assigned to the borrowers' file. This representative may be called upon to provide documents.

Escrow: A neutral third party who retains certain documents, money, deposits in real estate transactions who will deliver specific services upon fulfillment of certain conditions, as established in a written and signed contractual agreement.

Notary Public: One who is legally authorized to certify the authenticity of signatures and documents.

Current Mortgage Company: The borrowers' current lender. They will usually have their fees to close out (pay off) the current loan. Those fees will be added to the loan balance. The mortgage balance is always lower than the *pay-off* balance. The current mortgage company will typically add one-month's interest plus miscellaneous closing-out fees, plus any pre-payment penalties if applicable.

New Mortgage Company: The new lending institution that is financing the new loan.

County Recorder: An office held within the county that records Grant Deeds and Deeds of Trust.

Courier: One who has the responsibility of carrying and delivering official documents. Usually these documents are of value. These people are typically employed by a company but possibly may own their own courier business.

Hopefully you can now understand where some of your costs go when acquiring a loan. Each one of these players (positions) is in place to help you fund your loan. Your loan agent does not and *cannot* do all of the necessary functions in the loan process. They are simply one of many who play a part in the success of obtaining your loan. An additional role loan agents play outside their normal job description, is to be the voice and face of the process. Most banks employ such individuals and trust their loan agents will represent them in a very professional and ethical manner. Unfortunately, some banks or lending institutions are not so lucky, thus, the reason for this book.

THE LENGTH OF THE GAME:

The number one question a client seems to ask concerning the loan process is, "When will my loan close?" As a loan agent you want to close ALL your loans in a timely manner. One of the tricks to do this is to communicate with all the players involved. If you communicate with your players they can be more efficient in their role and keep the flow of the process going. It only takes one of the major players to drop the ball to hold up the loan process. A loan agent should try to never allow the mortgage finance game to go into overtime.

Trying to close a loan in a timely fashion can cause a high level of anxiety. There are a number of reasons why anxiety levels rise beside the fact the loan agents have to rely on a lot of other people to do their job properly. Maybe the client is one of influence and could refer a lot of business to them. Maybe the client is a family member and the loan agent wants everything to go smoothly to showcase their ability to do good work. Or, maybe their client is a real estate agent and the loan agent wants to make an impression to earn future business.

I remember clients of mine, the McIntoshes, were relocating from Federal Way, Washington, to Portland, Oregon. Mike McIntosh was a man of great influence. He was a Senior Pastor of a local church and greatly known within his community. Leaders in the United States have sought his counsel, and internationally he was often called upon for advice. Outside of who he was to all people, he and his wife Claire were great friends of my wife's and mine. Mike called one day and asked me if I could handle their loan and close it in about 10 days. Everything inside of me wanted to assure him it shouldn't be a problem. My friendship with this couple wanted the loan process to be flawless and trouble-free. However, I was honest with him. I explained it was possible but may be not probable. I explained we would shoot for his time frame, but we may need to file an extension if some unforeseen condition surfaced. He was very gracious and told me he understood the uniqueness of his request and if an extension had to be signed, he would do so. Nevertheless, my goal was to fund and record their loan within their time frame.

I got all my ducks in a row before the purchase and sale agreement got to me. I had preliminary discussions with key people in the process regarding their file. When the loan was submitted, we were off and running. Mike and Claire were prompt with any documents/information I needed. Within ten days their loan was funded.

Is that normal? Some banks would argue yes and some may argue no. There are banks out there that have stream-lined their back-end process so well, that if the loan agents had crossed their "t's" and dotted their "i's" and the files were properly documented, a 10-day funding would not be a problem.

For the most part, if a loan agent can close a loan within a three to four week period, it would be considered a good average amount of time. Can a loan take longer than four weeks? Absolutely. Just because a loan takes a little longer than usual, it doesn't necessarily mean your loan agent is causing the problem.

What causes a loan to go into overtime? (Answer: *Many potential reasons.*)

- ## The Loan Agent

When a borrower unfortunately falls into the hands of a Rookie Loan Agent or a Predatory Loan Agent, sometimes the loan will take a little longer. It could be because of in-nocent mistakes or sneaky business practices. A loan agent can be the cause of overtime.

- ## The Real Estate Agent

Everybody and his brother is now a real estate agent. When working with inexperienced agents, sometimes purchase and sale agreements are written up incorrectly. An incorrect purchase and sale agreement or an addendum to a purchase and sale agreement may cost valuable time. Most agents who work for reputable companies have a management team who carefully and meticulously guides their agents through all steps of the sales process, especially when writing up contracts. If there is an error, it is usually caught through the quality control process the real estate brokers have established for their office.

- ## Someone on the team other than your loan agent

You have to understand we are all human. None of us are exempt from making a mistake. Processors are vulnerable to submitting the client's file in the wrong loan program. It has happened before. A client could lose a week to two weeks depending on when the mistake was caught. Underwriting (U/W) turn times can be as long as five business days. When business picks up in the mortgage industry, a bottleneck effect can take place in the banks' U/W departments. Underwriters can get backed up. Throw in a weekend, or worst, a three or four-day holiday that falls on a weekend and U/W turn-times are at five *business* days. It could pencil out to be two weeks before your file is underwritten. You also have the potential of an appraiser taking longer than normal to get their estimate back to your loan agent. A current lender may not cooperate in getting the payoff figures to escrow. They may say it takes 10 business days to provide the needed information.

▪ The Client

Loan agents have to trust that what their clients are telling them is true. If clients are withholding information, they need to understand the truth will surface. The truth very well may change the original quoted interest rate and program. Re-submitting to another bank because the clients' scenario was wrong can put the mortgage finance game into overtime.

▪ The Subject Property

Sometimes the property itself can cause a loan to go into overtime. I had a client in southern California for whom we could not close on the loan within the desired timeframe. My client had signed, and in the eleventh hour the title company called the escrow company to let them know they found a $19,000 lien on the property. This lien was not on the property's preliminary report and had suddenly surfaced. When we asked about the lien, my client said it was from an old second mortgage that was paid off a couple years back. We all had to wait as my client located the old paperwork to show the loan was paid off. The time it took to retrieve the old documents and the time for the title company to review and make their corrections to the property's profile cost us time.

Once in awhile, a property does not appraise to the value that is needed. If property values come in lower, that may jeopardize your loan being approved. Loan agents may have to go back and re-structure the loan. Worst-case scenario, the loan will not be approved due to the actual determined appraised value.

Do not let these *"what if"* scenarios scare you. Good loan agents know the right questions to ask you and how to structure your loan. If they see any problems, they will tackle them in the beginning of the process. They will make any adjustments necessary before continuing. Working in this manner will help prevent any last minute surprises.

HOW THE GAME IS PLAYED:

Whenever I play a board game, I have to get out the instructions and read. In every game I play, there is always an order in which to play the game. First, roll the dice. Second, move your game piece around the board. Third, pull the corresponding card to the square you landed on. Fourth, follow the instructions on the card, etc. If you were to go out of order and pull a card before rolling the dice, the game would be out of order, and winning would not be valid.

The mortgage financing game has an order to it as well. You simply cannot jump straight to Docs if you have yet to submit your loan and acquired an approval. Here you are going to learn the basic steps which a client must take to acquire a loan.

Note: *These steps are generic by nature. Banks may differ in their process due to their designed infrastructure. A bank may have what could be considered an unconventional loan process. Do not be shocked if you work with a bank whose loan process is more streamlined than the following steps:*

Step 1: **Application process**

The clients must provide personal information to their loan agents. The loan agents will then do a comprehensive review. They will identify where the clients are currently in their credit standing and then qualify them with their new mortgage payment. This is the necessary first step.

Step 2: **Loan agent sends out disclosures** *(the initial set of paperwork to start the loan process).*

A checklist of items needed from the borrower may accompany this paperwork, such as income and asset verification, liability statements, bankruptcy papers, divorce decree, etc. The quicker the client signs and provides the requested information, the quicker the loan will close. They will also open escrow, open title (*request a preliminary title report on the subject property*), and order an appraisal if applicable.

Step 3: **Submission Process**

The loan package (*hopefully a complete file*) is sent to processing. The processor will handle the borrowers' file by organizing their information and making sure everything is ready for underwriting. Then the processor will submit the loan file to the appropriate bank. Banks' processing times may vary depending on how busy they are. Typically, a file should be in the processing stage no more than 48 hours.

What may hold up the file from being submitted is if the loan agent does not have a complete file. Different banks require different items when submitting a loan. If a loan agent does not have a complete file, the loan process may get backed up for the client.

Step 4: Underwriting the loan

An underwriter underwrites the loan. Underwriting turn-times may vary depending on their workload. They will often approve a loan, but request various conditions that need to be met/fulfilled prior to allowing the loan to go to Docs. These conditions may or may not involve the client's participation.

Step 5: Going to Docs

Once any prior-to-doc conditions are fulfilled, the client's docs are ordered. Usually the processors will order them. Once the Doc Drawer has prepared them (typically, within 24 hour period) they are forwarded to escrow.

Step 6: Signing the final paperwork

Escrow receives the docs via email or courier and prepares them for the actual signing of the loan. A good loan agent will review the final paperwork with escrow prior to the client signing them. The client signs the final paperwork.

Step 7: Funding process

The bank receives the signed paperwork. The loan is

assigned to a funder. If everything is correct with the signed paperwork and there are no outstanding conditions that need to be met before closing the loan, the funder releases funds to escrow to close and record the loan with the county.

Step 8: Closing of loan

Escrow receives the okay to fund. They wait for funds to come in by wire from the bank. They disperse funds according to the lender's instructions and record the loan with the county.

That is how the game is played in a nutshell. A good loan agent will anticipate what play comes next, and will act accordingly. The loan-processing game can be played, from start to finish, within 10 business days to four weeks. Any longer would be viewed as overtime.

YOUR POSITION AND WHAT IS EXPECTED OF YOU:

The clients' position is very simple, but yet can be very difficult for some people. The clients' role is to provide accurate information about themselves. Clients want the bank to fully disclose everything to them, and yet, at times, clients will *not* fully disclose everything to the bank about themselves. That smells like a double standard.

Clients cannot hide from the bank. Sometimes clients are afraid to fully disclose everything because they fear not qualifying for a loan. Loan agents are equally guilty if they sense or know something is wrong with their client, but try to push the loan through anyway. It never works. Truth about the clients' scenario will always surface. If there is something the client is hiding, the bank will figure it out. The only question is when?

The best advice any client can get is to be completely honest with your loan agents. Tell them everything. If you think something may disqualify you, bring it up. It will expose itself in the end anyway. Wouldn't you want to know in the beginning if you truly qualify? You do not want to waste emotional time and money on a process that is doomed to fail from the beginning. Banks have so many creative programs with equally creative underwriting guidelines. You may qualify for a loan; it is just that the loan agent may have to structure your deal a little differently to make it work. Honesty is always your best option. That is the most important function of your position within the mortgage financing game.

If you are stepping into the mortgage financing game or getting ready to, you will be part of a team. All the players on the team have a common goal: getting you a loan. We need to work with each other, not against each other. Loan agents need to be open and honest with their clients, and the clients need to be open and honest with them. With all players involved firing on all cylinders, your dream to mortgage a new home or refinance your current home can come true. I will leave you with this quote from Henry Ford, "Coming together is a beginning, keeping together is progress, working together is success."

Chapter

11

Valuing Your Loan Agent

There is one thing that is often overlooked when working with GOOD loan agents. That one thing is their value! The loan agents are valuable to their clients; even if the clients do not recognize it.

Dear Current or Future Homeowner:

I want to congratulate you in making it through to the end of this book. Out of all the chapters in this book, I would encourage you to really appreciate this last chapter, "Valuing Your Loan Agent." Hopefully you have been enlightened about what to look for in a lender, what goes on behind the scenes, your true costs within a loan, and asking the right questions the right way. Those chapters have probably been a real eye opener in more ways than one.

The one thing you need to understand is that this book is geared to protect you from *the predatory lender*, not to protect you from lenders in general. Not all lenders are bad. However, there are greedy loan agents out there, and they have given mortgage lending a bad name, making the honest lenders work ten times harder to prove their ethical intentions with their clients.

UnMasking the Mortgage Madness is to help you identify the early signs of being taken advantage of. After learning what you've learned, I still want to encourage you to not be gun shy when dealing with your next lender. The consumer should never fear loan agents in general. Mortgage lending is an honest way to make a good living, not at the expense of the consumer, but by providing an honest quality of service that gives people great hope and a great future as homeowners.

There is one thing that is often overlooked when working with GOOD loan agents. That one thing is their *value*! The loan agents are valuable to their clients; even if the clients do not recognize it.

Here is the Encarta® World English Dictionary definition of the word *value*.

1) The **worth**, **importance**, or **usefulness** of something to somebody.

2) To rate something according to its perceived **worth**, **importance**, or **usefulness**.

3) To **regard** somebody or something as **important** or **useful**.

When I read this definition these words jump out at me:

- Worth

- Importance

- Usefulness

If you are working with good loan agents who know their "*stuff*," you should value them. Value their importance and their usefulness. A good loan agent is useful for many things. One is being there for you and educating you about the process you are walking through. You should be grateful for their significant contribution to you acquiring a loan. It should be worth something to you.

Let's think about it for a moment. Mortgages are confusing! Have you ever wondered whether you were getting the best possible rates? Have you ever felt as if you just didn't know the right questions to ask? Have you ever compared your mortgage with that of friends' and wondered why they got a better deal? If we are honest, most of us have had those same thoughts or concerns at one time or another.

The reality is, mortgages are very confusing and continuously changing. There are dozens of types of loans and many structures within each type of loan. For the homeowner, the process of understanding which type of loan is best can be frustrating and overwhelming.

That is where good loan agents can be of value to you. They know how confusing this process can be and therefore, will go the extra mile in making it easier for you. Plus, admitting it or not, you do need them. You cannot walk yourself through the finance process. You wouldn't even know where to begin, whom to talk to, and what different programs to research. Value the importance of your loan agents' experience and expertise.

In 2001, I had laser eye surgery. It was probably one of the best decisions I've ever made. I had 20/40 vision in my right eye and 20/100 vision in my left eye. The Department of Motorized Vehicles considered me legally blind. I had to wear glasses at all times. When it came to choosing my doctor for this much anticipated procedure, I chose carefully. To my surprise, I actually did not spend a lot of time with my doctor. The time I spent with him was minimal. I had a couple of pre-op appointments and one or two post-op appointments. The appointments took just a few minutes. The procedure was remarkably quick. My right eye was finished in about eight seconds and my left eye was done in seven seconds. That was it. Roughly 30 minutes of one-on-one time with this doctor. The bill was $1,500. I spent a total of about a half hour with this man and gave him $1,500. That equates to $3,000 an hour! Who makes $3,000 an hour (*besides him*)?

Here's the thing, I'd pay it again in a second if I had to. Why? VALUE. That doctor was a trained professional. He took intricate measurements, made precise cuts, prescribed appropriate medications, and provided the needed follow-up to assure I was properly taken care of. This doctor was an incredibly important person in my life. He was able to provide a life-changing experience for me that I could not do on my own. I had to trust that every decision he made was in my best interest.

He gave me my eyesight back. When I was finished I went from being considered legally blind to having 20/15 vision in both eyes.

In many ways loan agents provide a similar value of service. They provide services that you cannot obtain without their expertise and knowledge.

Knowledgeable loan agents bring tremendous value to all your mortgage transactions. The loan agents stay up to speed on the ever-changing world of mortgages. They are the experts that represent your best interests to potential lenders. They get compensated to serve *you* as your financial advocate. They will cultivate a relationship with you and develop an acute understanding of your individual needs. Their job is to find the right loan that works for you. They will negotiate on your behalf to get your loan approved. The loan agent will become one of your most valuable friends in the home purchasing and/or refinancing process. If you need help in repairing your credit, a good loan agent knows how to best communicate with lenders and leaves no stone unturned to provide you with every conceivable opportunity to obtain that loan.

I've always said, there is no such thing as a free lunch, but there is such a thing as a FAIR lunch. My experience has been that people understand that good service comes with a fair price. No one wants to be overcharged or cheated. Hopefully, you're not looking for the *free* deal, either. It simply doesn't exist. You've heard the old saying, "If it sounds too good to be true, chances are it is not true." And that is certainly the case with mortgages. When a mortgage is advertised as "free," nine times out of ten the fees are simply getting packed into your interest rate — shifting from one pocket to another. There are rare occasions when it makes sense to do just that, but for the most part, it's really poor stewardship of your money. And as previously mentioned that "free" loan, might end up costing you more than double your original closing costs.

Remember my definition of integrity:

Doing what is best for someone else, when another decision would be best for you.

Not only does it apply to the loan agent, but to you, the consumer, as well. What would ultimately be best for you is to get a loan truly for free. However, people would starve if they did business for free. Use integrity with your loan agent. *UnMasking the Mortgage Madness* is designed to protect you from being overcharged and misled. It's not meant to *discourage* you from paying a just and fair compensation for the unique services a loan agent will provide.

Hopefully, you feel you have been provided with some vital information and some secrets about the mortgage industry that the predatory loan agent does not want you to know. My desire is that these secrets you have learned will save you potentially thousands of dollars in closing costs.

If you currently mortgage a home or you are looking to mortgage your first home here shortly, you are considered what is known as a mortgager. With any luck, *UnMasking the Mortgage Madness* has made you into a WISE mortgager and not allowed you to remain an uniformed mortgager.

You have taken a big step toward empowering yourself to recognize predatory lending. May this book arm you with the tools necessary to obtain the best possible mortgage for you and your family.

We all make investments in our lives. In most cases, our home is our biggest financial investment. The investment in this book will truly save you not just once but also potentially multiple times as you buy and refinance homes.

May all your future home financing decisions be made by a new, educated YOU!

Sincerely,

Rick Bulman
Your Trusted Mortgage Advisor

Glossary

Glossary of Common Mortgage Terms

"A" Credit

A consumer who is considered low risk. One with a very good credit rating. This consumer often gets the best interest rates, programs, and costs.

Acceleration Clause

A section in a contractual document that authorizes the lender to exercise the right to demand payment of the full loan balance if the borrower violates one or more clauses in the note.

Accrued Interest

Much like negative amortization, where interest is incurred but not paid each month. The interest is added to the amount still owed.

Adjustable Rate Mortgage (ARM)

A loan program in which the interest rate changes, typically after a predetermined fixed period.

Adjustment Interval

The "time" between the interest rate and/or monthly payment changes on an Adjustable Rate Mortgage. Usually, these periods of time are six months or one, three, five, seven or ten years.

Affordability

The consumer's determined maximum amount financed, based on income and liabilities.

Agreement of Sale

A contractual agreement signed by the buyer and seller stating the terms and conditions concerning the property being sold. Also referred to as the Purchase and Sale Agreement.

Alt-A

A mortgage classification pertaining to a certain risk factor. Placed between "A" paper conforming and sub-prime risk cliental. Also known as "A minus" paper.

Alternative Documentation

A different approached to confirm a borrower's income and employment without having to wait for verification sent by third parties. This expedites the process, because the lender will accept paycheck stubs, W-2s, and the borrower's original bank statements.

Amortization (concerning mortgages)

A repayment method of debt owed on a mortgage through scheduled monthly payments.

Amortization Schedule

A table or schedule that shows the breakdown of payments paying off the loan.

Amount Financed

The actual amount (loan amount) being financed less any down payments being made. If the sales price is $100,000 and a down payment of $10,000 was applied, the "amount financed" is $90,000.

Annual Percentage Rate (APR)

Also known as APR, reflects the cost of a mortgage as a yearly rate. The APR is likely to be higher than the interest rate that dictates the mortgage payment, as it takes into account points and other closing costs. The APR reveals the "true cost of a loan" by giving the homebuyer an opportunity to compare the mortgage loan and its costs with other lending offers.

Application

A document filled out by or on behalf of an applicant who is applying for a loan.

Application Fee

A fee that is sometimes charged by a lender when borrowers fill out an application.

Appraisal

A written report prepared by an appraiser that estimates a property's current market value.

Appraiser

A qualified individual who through education, training, and experience provides appraisals.

Appraisal Fee

A fee charged by an appraiser for a written report on a particular property.

Approval

The acceptance of the borrower's loan application once the file has been underwritten by an underwriter.

Assumable Loan

Loan programs whereby a creditworthy purchaser may assume the mortgage contract of the seller.

Authorized User

When the primary holder of a credit card authorizes someone else to use the card. Authorized users are not responsible for paying any charges on the primary cardholder's credit card bill.

Automated Underwriting

The process of using a computer program to evaluate borrower's risk. This program may instruct the lender to forward the file to an actual underwriter to manually underwrite the file. This computer program can usually let borrowers know their qualification standings within minutes.

Bait and Switch

When borrowers are told one thing to get them in the door, and the reality of their situation turns out to be much different than they thought.

Balance

The unpaid sum of a loan.

Balloon

A large, lump-sum payment being called for and made after regularly scheduled smaller mortgage payments have been made. This payment pays the loan balance in full bringing the loan to maturity. Example, a 30 due in 15 (written as 30/15 or 360/180) is a mortgage payment that reflects a 30-year term payment, but is called to be paid in full on the 15th year anniversary.

Bi-Weekly Mortgage

A mortgage in which the borrower pays half of the monthly payment every two weeks.

Bridge Loan

A short-term loan, used until the buyers sell their current home, which helps "bridge" the period between the closing date of the new home and the closing date of the home being sold.

Buy-Down

The ability to permanently buy down the interest rate through the payment of points.

Buying Agent

One that acts for or represents the buyer in a sales transaction.

Cash-Out Refi

When re-doing (refinancing) an existing loan, the homeowner borrows more money than the original loan balance to get cash for: home improvements, paying bills (debt consolidation), or miscellaneous use.

Closing

The completion of a loan or a transaction. In particular, concerning contracts that are signed transferring ownership of real estate.

Closing Costs

Fees and charges that are incurred by the borrower from a lender that exceed the sale price of a home or for a refinance, for services rendered. Also, fees and charges incurred by the seller that come from the general cost of selling a home.

Closing Date

The date on which the purchase or refinance is final and the loan transaction closes. On a purchase, this date is typically pre-determined.

Co-Borrowers

An additional individual(s) who signs the note and is equally responsible for the mortgage payments being made. Typically this person is married to the borrower.

Co-Mortgager

An additional individual(s) who signs the note and is equally responsible for the mortgage payments being made. Typically this person is NOT married to the borrower.

Conforming Loan

Loan programs that have guidelines that conform to Fannie Mae and Freddie Mac guidelines.

Construction Loan

A short-term temporary loan that finances the construction of buildings or homes. The financing is usually advanced to the builder as work progresses. Once the construction is finished, a permanent loan is used to pay off the short-term interim construction loan.

Contingency

Concerning the purchase of a home, a condition that must be fulfilled before a contract is legally binding before the close of escrow.

Conventional Loan

Any loan program that is secured by a mortgage or deed of trust that is not insured or guaranteed by an agency of the federal government. These agencies are known as FHA or VA.

Conversion Option

When an Adjustable Rate Mortgage carries the option to convert to a Fixed Rate Mortgage at a predetermined point of the loan.

Correspondent Lending

A bank, broker, or financial institution that does the work in place of another financial institution where a transaction will occur after the closing of a loan. The bank, broker, or financial institution will deliver/sell the loan(s) to the other, typically much larger financial institution.

COSI

Cost Of Savings Index. One of numerous interest rate indices used to determine interest rate adjustments concerning adjustable rate mortgages.

Co-Signing a Note

One who assumes responsibility for the borrower's loan in the event the borrower defaults in their mortgage payments.

Credit Report

A report from a credit bureau containing detailed information bearing on credit-worthiness, including the individual's credit history.

Credit Score

A report that reveals how one is doing concerning paying bills on time. Three bureaus will grade the credit worthiness of an individual (Trans Union, Equifax, and Experian). Each bureau gives a numerical score, based on an individual's credit history. The scores are referred to as FICO scores. FICO was originated by Fair Issac Co.

Debt Consolidation

Typically taking place in a refinance. A borrower finances more than the current loan balance and utilizes equity to take cash out and pay debts off, making it part of the new mortgage loan.

Debt to Income Ratio (DTI)

A measure that compares debt payments to the gross income generated. This measure is referred to as a percentage, which gives lenders a pulse on the likelihood of the borrower's ability to make the mortgage payments. Also known as "qualifying ratios."

Deed

A legal record whereby title to a particular property is transferred from one owner to another. This document contains a description of the property and is signed, witnessed, and delivered to the buyer once the sale is final.

Deed of Trust

A deed that is documented in public records. This deed conveys there is a lien held on the subject property. A deed of trust is often used in place of a mortgage. When the debt is paid in full, the deed is canceled.

Deed in Lieu of Foreclosure

When a homeowner, having a hard time making the mortgage payment prepares a quitclaim deed, that transfers the homeowner's property rights to the lender. Some lenders may accept ownership of the property this way without receiving money owed. This is used as an alternative to having the lender foreclose on the property.

Default

When a homeowner fails to honor the commitment to make the mortgage payment.

Deferred Interest

When the loan balance grows because the mortgage payment does not quite cover the monthly interest. This is sometimes referred to as "negative amortization."

Delinquency

When a borrower allows the mortgage payment, by way of default, to exceed 30 days.

Demand, The

A mortgage note that the lender can call due at any time without prior notice. An actual statement of the current loan that indicates what is required to pay off in full.

Direct Lender

The actual financial institution that disburses funds to the borrower at the closing.

Disclosures

The initial set of paperwork the loan agent sends to the client to start the loan process. These papers disclose the nature of the loan, as well as the estimated cost of the loan. These papers need to be signed and returned to the loan agent.

Discount Points

A fee or charge that equals one percent of the loan amount. Discount Points on the Good Faith Estimate are used to buy down the interest rate. They are prepaid interest costs. The more points, the lower the interest rate. It is NOT always a good idea to buy down the interest rate. It has been proven to be a case-by-case basis. Also referred to as "points."

Doc Drawer

Those who draw (prepare) the final documentation the borrower signs at the closing of the loan. They prepare the docs, along with any instructions from the lender to escrow. They then forward by (usually) email or overnight delivery to escrow.

Documentation Requirements

Each lender/loan program calls for certain documents that must be presented by the borrower when applying for a mortgage. These documents help assess the prospective client's qualifications. Different loan programs may call for different documentation.

Document Review

When a lender reviews documents necessary to fund a loan. There is typically a charge for such services.

Down Payment

A dollar amount or percentage of the sales price paid up front by the buyer that reduces the amount of the loan or mortgage.

Due-On-Sale Clause

A clause that states if the property is sold, the loan must be paid in full through the proceeds of the sale.

Earnest Money

A deposit a buyer makes toward a purchase as evidence of good faith when the purchase and sale agreement is signed.

Equity

In connection with a home, the difference between the value of the home and the balance of outstanding mortgage loans on the home.

Escrow

A neutral third party who retains certain documents, money, deposits in real estate transactions who will deliver specific services upon fulfillment of certain conditions, as established in a written and signed contractual agreement.

Fallout

When a loan application has been withdrawn or cancelled because the borrowers have changed their minds for one reason or another.

Fannie Mae

One of two federal agencies that is a secondary-mortgage market company that purchases home loans from lenders (the other is Freddie Mac).

Fees

The charges the borrower incurs from the lender and all third party entities when applying for a home loan.

FHA Loans

FHA = Federal Housing Administration. A government agency whose main objective is to underwrite residential mortgage loans. The FHA loan requires mortgage insurance and offers low down payment possibilities. There are loan amount limits on FHA loans.

FICO Score

A report that reveals how one is doing concerning paying bills on time. Three bureaus will grade the credit worthiness of an individual (Trans Union, Equifax, and Experian). Each bureau gives a numerical score based on an individual's credit history. The scores are referred to as FICO scores. FICO was originated by Fair Issac Co.

Financing Points

When a borrower includes paying points in the loan amount, rolling the closing costs into the loan.

First Mortgage

A mortgage that is in first position and has priority to be paid off before all other mortgages and liens.

Fixed Rate Mortgage (FRM)

A mortgage where the interest rate is decided in the beginning and fixed for the entire term of the loan.

Floating Interest Rates

A loan program that has a variable interest rate. The rate adjustments are tied to a certain money-market indices.

Foreclosure

The legal process in which a lender takes action to acquire the home-owner's property because the borrower defaults on the mortgage payments.

Forbearance Agreement

A written repayment agreement between a lender and the borrower that contains a plan to reinstate a loan that is a minimum of three payments behind. This plan helps in rectifying the borrower's delinquent status.

Freddie Mac

One of two federal agencies that is a secondary-mortgage market company that purchases home loans from lenders (the other is Fannie Mae).

Fully Amortizing Loan

A loan in which the borrower makes principal and interest payments through regular installments to repay in full the mortgage debt incurred by the time the loan's term ends.

Fully Indexed Rate

Considered the actual interest rate, which is composed of the current index value plus the margin.

Funder

One who does the final checks and balances of the loan documents after the borrower has signed the final paperwork. Once all the lenders' conditions are met/satisfied, the funds will be released to close the borrowers' loan.

Gift of Equity

When a house sells below market value, and the difference between the sales price and the actual value amount is credited/considered a gift from the sellers to the buyers. Some lenders may allow the gift to count as down payment. Lenders have their own set of rules and guidelines concerning gift of equity.

Good Faith Estimate

A form that lists the estimated closing costs the borrower will incur at time of closing. This form is only an estimate. This is one of a few forms the lender is obligated to provide the borrower within three business days of receiving the loan application.

Grace Period

An additional period of time during which the lender allows a borrower to make payment on a debt without enforcing any penalty.

Graduated Payment Mortgage (GPM)

A mortgage in which the initial payment is lower than the fixed-rate mortgage. The payment will increase by a certain percentage for a specified time. (i.e., 3, 5, or 7 years). After the adjustment period, the loan payments will level out and become fixed.

Graduation Period

The time during which the payment rises on a Graduated Payment Mortgage.

Graduation Rate

The time when the interest rate will increase, which in turn will increase the payment on the Graduated Payment Mortgage.

Gross Income

Total income prior to taxes or expenses being deducted.

Hazard Insurance

Insurance that is required by every lender that will protect the property against any loss from fire or other hazards. This is also known as "homeowner's insurance." A lender will not lend on any property that is not insured.

Historical Scenario

A way to gauge or predict the future activity of how the index will adjust concerning ARM programs, based on past or historical patterns.

Homebuyer Protection Plan

A plan that claims to protect FHA homebuyers against any property defects.

Homeowner's Equity

The difference between the current market value of a home and the homeowner's current mortgage loan balance. Example: If the property is valued at $250,000 and the homeowner's mortgage balance is $155,000, there is $95,000 in equity.

Homeowner's Insurance

Insurance that is required by every lender that will protect the property against any loss from fire or other hazards. This is also known as "hazard insurance." A lender will not lend on any property that is not insured.

Home Equity Line of Credit (HELOC)

A line of credit that a borrower takes out against existing equity. The borrower will use this credit line like a credit card. This is considered a "second mortgage." The borrower only pays on what is used, not on the total credit line limit.

Home Equity Conversion Mortgage (HECM)

When a homeowner borrows money against their equity and receives monthly payments from the lender. This is also known as a "reverse mortgage."

Home Equity Line

Same as a Home Equity Line of Credit. Also may be referred to as "Equity Line."

Home Equity Loan

Not to be confused with a Home Equity Line. Home Equity Loan is not a line of credit. This is typically a fixed rate second mortgage on the property. This loan is considered to be in second position to be paid off if the subject property is sold or if the borrower defaults on the mortgage payments and a foreclosure takes place.

Housing Bubble

A term used when a rapid increase of real estate property values takes place. This is also known as the real estate bubble and property bubble.

HUD1 Form

A form that is used that itemizes ALL the charges the borrower will incur on the loan. This is to not be mistaken for the Good Faith Estimate clients receive in the beginning of the application process. This form is more exact and given to the borrower at signing.

Hybrid ARM

A variation of the Adjustable Rate Mortgage in which the loan carries a fixed portion in the beginning of the loan's life for a certain period of time before the loan begins to adjust.

Impounds

Also known as an escrow or reserve account. If a borrower elects to have their taxes and insurance included in their mortgage payment, the bank will impound (set-up a reserve account) and will expect a certain amount of months collected upfront for property taxes and hazard (homeowner's) insurance. This process of collecting these funds upfront is known as impounding.

Indexed ARM

An ARM in which the interest rate adjustments are affected directly by a specific index in the market. When the index changes, the interest rate changes; therefore, the mortgage payment adjusts.

Initial Interest Rate

The beginning or starting interest rate that is fixed for a certain period of time on an ARM. The fixed period can be months or even the first few years of the loan.

Initial Rate Period

The initial period of time during which the interest rate does not change. These fixed periods of time are anywhere from a month to ten years.

Interest-Only Mortgage

A mortgage in which the borrower's monthly payment consists of paying only the monthly interest on the loan. There is no principle reduction that takes place. The interest-only option of payment is set for certain periods. Each loan program that offers the interest-only feature has its different set periods.

Interest Payment

The monthly dollar amount requested by the lender set to cover only the monthly interest portion of the loan.

Interest Rate

Concerning a home mortgage, a rate defined as a percentage charged to the borrower by the lender for borrowing funds to purchase a home.

Interest Rate Adjustment Period

The regularity of when the interest rate will adjust on an ARM. This adjustment period takes place after any fixed period portions of the loan have expired.

Interest Rate Ceiling

This is also known as a "life cap." It is the maximum adjustment the interest rate will increase on a particular ARM. The borrower will not experience the interest rate exceeding past the set life cap or interest ceiling cap.

Interest Rate Floor

The maximum adjustment decrease the interest rate will go on a particular ARM. The borrower will not experience the interest rate decreasing past the floor cap.

Interest Rate Decrease Cap

This controls how much the ARMs will adjust during their adjustment period. This cap sets allowable limits on the decrease of an ARM's interest rate. These caps will differ among adjustable rate loan programs.

Interest Rate Increase Cap

This controls how much the ARMs will adjust during their adjustment period. This cap sets allowable limits on the increase of an ARM's interest rate. These caps will differ between adjustable rate loan programs.

Internet Mortgages

When a borrower acquires a loan whereby most of the communication and process is done through the internet.

Investor

Concerning residential real estate, one who buys property as an investment, but does not intend to occupy such properties. Most investors intended to rent out to tenants.

IO

A short way of communicating a monthly mortgage payment that is an interest-only payment.

Jumbo Loan

A mortgage loan wherein the loan amount exceeds conforming loan limits set by Fannie Mae and Freddie Mac. The "Jumbo" loan amounts may change annually.

Junk Fees

A derogatory term where lenders, predatory-type lenders, add additional unnecessary fees to pad their bottom line. This type of charging is frowned upon and always at the borrower's expense.

Joint Tenants

The ownership of property by two or more persons. In the event of one owner's dying, the surviving owner receives the deceased's share of the property.

Late Fees

A fee that is charged by a lender once the grace period has expired. Most mortgage grace periods are 10 to 15 days. Example: payment is due on the first of the month for $1,000. The grace period will let the borrower pay $1,000 up to the 15th of the month. On the 16th, a late charge (which varies) will be applied to the monthly payment.

Late Payment

A payment made once the "grace period" has expired. The borrower's credit will not be hurt unless the payment is not received in full by the first of the following month.

Lease-To-Own Purchase

A transaction in which a prospective buyer leases a home from the seller with the option to purchase the home at a specific time.

Lender

The actual finance institution that lends the funds to the borrower at the time of closing.

Lien

A form of security that is placed on a property to ensure that the leinee will receive a payment of debt. Lenders have the right to act as leinees in order to claim the borrower's property in the event the borrower defaults.

Limited Cash-Out Refinance

The borrower refinances the loan and desires to get a little cash out for various reasons.

Loan Amount

The amount of money one borrows and promises to pay back. The loan amount is stated in the contractual agreement between the lender and the borrower.

Loan Discount Fee

Also known as "Points" and "Discount Points." This is fee charged to buy down the interest rate. It can be found on all GFE's right below the origination fee.

Loan Officer

An employee of a lending institution who originates loans for their company. Often referred to as Loan Agents, Mortgage Bankers, Account Executives, etc. Loan officers will often counsel and direct the borrower to the appropriate loan program.

Loan Provider

The actual lender (bank or institution) or mortgage broker who is providing the loan for the borrower.

Loan-To-Value Ratio (LTV)

The loan amount divided by the appraised value. Example: Loan amount of $200,000 ÷ Appraised value of $285,000 = 70% Loan-To-Value or 70% LTV.

Lock

An option whereby the borrower elects to secure the quoted interest rate by the lender through locking the rate. Lock periods vary anywhere from 15 days on up.

Lock Commitment Letter

A form all loan agents should receive when they lock the borrower's interest rate. This form discloses the interest rate that was locked, the day the rate was locked, when the lock expires, and any rebates (if not at PAR) being made by the loan agent.

Lock Failure

When a lender does not honor the interest rate the borrower believed to be locked. Sometimes factors change in the loan, and the lender is unable to honor the lock because certain aspects have changed concerning the loan/borrower's scenario.

Lock Period

The number of days a loan agent locks the borrower's interest rate. The longer the lock period, typically the higher the price for the interest rate.

LOE

Letter of Explanation. These letters often are requested from borrowers for various reasons: finances, past credit issues, employment, AKAs, etc.

Mandatory Disclosure

Also known as "Full Disclosure." Lenders are bound by RESPA (see RESPA for definition) law to disclose key documents to their prospective borrowers three days after an application is taken and credit is pulled.

Manufactured Housing

A house that is built off site in a factory and then delivered to the subject's property address.

Margin

A percentage amount added to the index (which can be anywhere from 2 to 3 percent) to make up the fully indexed rate on an ARM.

Maturity

When the last payment is made on a loan, the loan is considered to have "matured."

Maximum Loan Amount

Particular loan programs that have maximum loan amount restrictions. Some loan programs are only permitted to go up to certain dollar amounts. One example is government loans (FHA and VA).

Maximum Loan To Value (LTV) Ratio

Certain loan programs have LTV restrictions. They are limited by various factors. For an example, sub-prime loans have higher LTV allowances than the conforming Fannie Mae and Freddie Mac loan programs. Loan amounts may affect the LTV requirements. Jumbo loans linked with a borrower's credit rating may require the LTV to be low in order to qualify the borrower.

Maximum Lock

The longest period that the lender will lock the interest rate for the borrower. The most common maximum lock period is 60 days. Some banks based on loan programs will allow a borrower to lock up to 90 days. Rarely do lock maximums exceed a 90-day period. If they do, sometimes there is a cost to do so. The longer the lock, the greater the risk for the lender.

Minimum Down Payment

The minimum dollar amount or percentage amount allowed for a down payment dictated by a financial institution and/or loan program guidelines.

Monthly Housing Expense

The monthly costs associated with the borrower's mortgage loan. More specific to: Principal, Interest, Taxes, and Insurance (PITI). Other monthly costs also include any maintenance fees where applicable (e.g., condominiums, cooperatives, Planned Unit Developments, or Homeowners Associations).

Mortgage

A written document used in securing a property. This document serves as evidence for the lien on a specific property by a lender. The term "mortgage" or "mortgage loan" is often referred to both the lien and the loan.

Mortgage Bank

A mortgage company.

Mortgage Broker

An independent contractor sometimes referred to as "the middleman" between the lender and the borrower who shops wholesale lenders for wholesale interest rates and loan programs. The mortgage broker walks the borrower through the application process, submits the loan, and sends it to the lender for underwriting, but does not fund the loan.

Mortgage Company

A company known for selling all the loans they originate in the secondary market. Some companies may or may not service the loans they originate.

Mortgage Insurance

An insurance policy geared to protect the lender in the event of the borrower's defaulting on the loan. This is an insurance policy that benefits the lender but not the borrower. The borrower is liable for all the monthly insurance premiums.

Mortgage Insurance Premium

The initial up front charge the borrower pays at closing. Also, known for the monthly insurance installments the borrower is liable for. These installments are part of the mortgage payment, not billed separately.

Mortgage Insurance Cancellation

The act of canceling a mortgage insurance policy, primarily through a refinance or sale of the home. In some cases, a bank may drop the mortgage insurance if an updated appraisal is given showing the home has a new LTV of 80% or lower. Every bank has its own unique policy when it comes to mortgage insurance cancellations.

Mortgage Lender

The financial entity that disburses funds to the borrower at the time of closing.

Mortgage Payment

The principle and interest payment made by the borrower.

Mortgage Scams

Deceptive behavior by people who would be considered predatory lenders. Through manipulation they acquire loans and use the borrowers' lack of understanding against them. They grow their bottom line at the borrowers' expense.

Mortgage Shopping

When a prospective client goes to various lenders to compare interest rates and programs. The client's goal is to find the best deal for the family's needs.

Negative Amortization

Much like "accrued interest," where interest is incurred but not paid each month. The interest is added to the amount still owed.

Negative Amortization Cap

The maximum amount an ARM loan program will allow a loan balance to go into a negative amortization (an increased loan balance).

Negative Homeowners Equity

When the borrower owes more on their home than what is actually owed on the home loan.

Net Branch

When (typically larger) lenders allow mortgage brokers to work under their umbrella as an employee. However, the mortgage broker still retains independence as a broker.

No-Cost Mortgage

When the lender and/or the seller of the subject property being purchased pays the majority of the closing costs. Borrowers who acquire "No-Cost" mortgage/loan usually finance their fees into their interest rate. Thus, the way many lenders claim to pay for their fees.

Non-Conforming Mortgage

A mortgage that does not conform to Fannie Mae and Freddie Mac loan program guidelines.

Non-Permanent Resident Alien

A non-citizen who is a green card holder and is employed in the US.

No Asset Loan

A loan program where the verification of the borrower's assets are not required by the lender.

No Cash-Out/Rate and Term Refinance

When a borrower refinances simply to lower the interest rate and mortgage payment with no desire to pull money out for any other reasons.

No Income Loan

A loan program where the verification of the borrower's income is not required by the lender.

Non-Warrantable Condo

A condominium that does not meet the lender's specific requirements.

No Ratio Loan

A loan program where the borrower's DTI ratio is not factored in the loan.

Note

Something in writing that serves as evidences to a debt that is promised by another individual to pay.

Option ARM

An adjustable rate mortgage that offers four payment options to the borrower. The four payment options are: A minimum payment (which carries the negative amortization possibility), Interest-only, 30-year, and the 15-year payment. The minimum payment adjusts annually with a 7.5% payment cap. The other three options adjust monthly according to what the index is doing. The type of Option Arm program one gets will determine the index to which it is tied.

Origination Fee

A charge by the loan agent for originating the loan.

Payment Increase Cap

A cap that affects/protects the monthly payment from exceeding the specific loan program guideline for the ARM loan. This cap keeps the payment from increasing too high.

Payment Decrease Cap

A cap that affects the monthly payment from decreasing beyond the specific loan program guideline for the ARM loan. This cap keeps the payment from decreasing below the floor rate.

Payment Period

The entire period during which the borrower is obligated to make payments.

Payment Shock

A larger monthly mortgage payment than the borrower is accustomed to making. A lot of banks are conscious of the payment shock percentage when a client goes from renting to owning a home. Some programs have a payment shock clause. Some sub-prime banks on their interest-only programs have a 100% payment shock stipulation. The borrower cannot exceed 100% payment shock for a particular loan program. Example: Borrower rents for $1,000/month. The new home costs $2,000/month. That equals 100% payment shock.

Payoff Month

The month the borrower pays the loan off and brings it to maturity.

Pay-Off Statement

An actual statement of the current loan that indicates what is required to pay off in full.

Per Diem Interest

Interest from the day of closing to the first day of the following month that the borrower is required to pay.

Permanent Buydown

When a borrower pays points to reduce the interest rate. This option may make sense to do at times.

PI

A short way of communicating a monthly mortgage payment that is principal and interest only.

Piggyback

When two mortgage loans are closing concurrently. Typically, an 80% first mortgage and a 5%, 10%, 15%, or 20% second mortgage. These loan combinations are specified usually this way: 80/5/15, 80/10/10, 80/15/5, and 80/20/0. Piggybacks are useful, as they keep the borrower from having to pay mortgage insurance.

PIT

A short way of communicating a monthly mortgage payment that is principal, interest, and taxes only.

PITI

A short way of communicating a monthly mortgage payment that consists of principal, interest, taxes, and insurance.

PMI

Stands for Private Mortgage Insurance.

Points

A fee or charge that equals one percent of the loan amount. Points or Discount Points are on the Good Faith Estimate and are used to buy down the interest rate. They are prepaid interest costs. The more points one pays, the lower the interest rate one can get. It is NOT always a good idea to buy down the interest rate. It has been proven to be a case-by-case basis.

Portfolio Lender

Lenders who do not sell the loans they originate, as they are part of their specific portfolio.

Pre-Approval

A loan commitment by a lender on behalf of the prospective borrower. Most pre-approvals are subject to property inspection and verification of the borrower's personal information. Also referred to as a "pre-qualification."

Predatory Lending

An array of unethical lender practices designed to take advantage of innocent borrowers.

Pre-Lim

Abbreviation for Preliminary Report. A report generated by the title company that discloses information about the subject property, such as who is on title, property taxes, any liens against the property, etc.

Pre-Payment

Often referred to as an extra mortgage payment that is made above and beyond the regularly scheduled mortgage payments.

Pre-Payment Penalty (PPP)

A penalty charge from the lender to the borrower for paying off a loan prior to an agreed upon (specific) time. This charge can equal up to six months' worth of interest. There are many different types of pre-payment penalties. Note: Do not agree to a loan where the PPP exceeds the fixed portion of an ARM loan. Example: A client has a two-year fixed ARM with a three-year PPP. The loan is fixed for the first two years but will adjust monthly come year three. The client is trapped for year three waiting for the PPP to be up, all the while living with an adjustable rate mortgage that may be going up and up.

Pre-Qualification

A loan commitment by a lender on behalf of the prospective borrower. Most pre-qualifications are subject to property inspection and verification of the borrower's personal information. Also referred to as a "pre-approval."

Price-Gouging

When a lender charges interest rates and/or fees that are excessive compared to what the same borrowers could find if they shopped to another mortgage company.

Primary Residence

Where the borrower primarily lives.

Principal

The portion of the monthly payment that reduces the loan balance.

Private Mortgage Insurance

Mortgage insurance provided by private mortgage insurance companies.

Processing

A series of actions or operations that takes place prior to underwriting. Includes files organization and other administrative functions required prior to final underwriting.

Profit and Loss Statement

A document that reveals the sales, expenses, and profits and any loss of profits over a period of time.

Property Taxes

A tax assessment produced by the county, based usually on the value of the property.

Qualification

The process a loan agent walks prospective borrowers through to determine whether they have the ability and means to pay back their loan.

Qualifying Rate

The interest rate used to qualify the prospective borrowers, which will affect their monthly mortgage payment.

Qualifying Ratios

A measure that compares people's debt payments to their gross income. This measure is referred in a percentage, which gives lenders a pulse on the likelihood of the borrowers' ability to make their mortgage payments. The guidelines require the loan agent to factor in the new PITI and all other liabilities coupled with the borrowers' income. See DTI for equation.

Qualification Requirements

Loan program guidelines by lenders that dictate certain conditions for loan approvals. These conditions are often referred to as qualification requirements.

Rate

Abbreviated version of "interest rate."

Rate/Point Breakeven

The break even period in order for it to be profitable to pay points to reduce the interest rate.

Rate Sheets

A chart of interest rates with points, known in the mortgage world as prices; each point or price is attached to the particular rates located on the chart. The lender prepares the rate sheet.

Rebate

An incentive paid by the bank to the broker/loan agent based on the interest rate that is sold to the client. The higher the interest rate, the more rebate. Rebate is also known as or referred to as "Yield Spread Premium" (YSP).

Recasting

When an ARM re-amortizes itself to protect itself from additional negative amortization. Recasting periods are usually predetermined in the loan program guidelines.

Reconveyance

When a property is transferred back to the owner after a mortgage is fully repaid.

Refinance

Paying off an old loan (existing mortgage) while at the same time financing the new mortgage. The new mortgage proceeds pay off the old or current loan.

Required Cash to Close

The total cash required of the homebuyer to bring in to signing at time of closing. These funds should include down payment and any and all closing costs.

Reserve Account

Refer to Impounds.

RESPA

The Real Estate Settlement Procedures Act, a Federal consumer protection statute first enacted in 1974. This act protects the borrowers by making the lenders disclose certain documents that reveal the reality of what they are getting in way of a loan program, as well as what they are being charged.

Retail Lender

A lender (typically a bank) that works directly with the public and offers them loan programs.

Reverse Mortgage

A loan geared for the elderly homeowners in which they borrow money from their equity and receive it in monthly installments as a source of income. Their balance rises over time. The money received in monthly installments is not called to be repaid until the owner dies, sells the house, or moves out permanently.

RHS

RHS is short for Rural Housing Services, which is part of the U.S. Department of Agriculture. They offer minimal down payment and guarantee loans for rural residence.

Right of Rescission

The borrower's right to cancel their refinance within three days of closing. If the borrower is refinancing the primary residence. Investments properties and purchases do not have a three-day right of rescission.

Scheduled Mortgage Payment

The amount the borrower is scheduled to pay set by the lender.

Second Mortgage

A fixed rate mortgage that owners take out on their property. This loan is considered to be in second position to be paid off if the subject property is sold or if the borrowers default on their mortgage payments and a foreclosure takes place.

Secondary Markets

Markets where mortgage loans are sold from one institution to another.

Self-Employed Borrower

Borrowers who own their own businesses. They usually provide documents such as income tax returns rather than information provided by an employer. Most of the time the self-employed borrower tries to qualify on a stated loan program.

Selling Agent

One that acts for or represents the seller in a sales transaction.

Seller Contribution

A seller contributes toward a borrower's down payment or closing costs.

Servicing

When an institution handles the administrative portion of the loan once it is sold on the secondary market. These administrative duties include collecting monthly payments, maintaining records of loan progress, assuring payments of taxes and insurance, and pursuing delinquent accounts.

Servicing Agent

The institution that services a loan. This institution may or may not be the lender who originated the borrower's loan.

Servicing Transfer

When another replaces one who is servicing a loan.

Settlement Costs

Fees and charges that are incurred by the borrower from a lender that exceed the sales price of a home or for a refinance. Fees and charges incurred by the seller that come from the general cost of selling a home. Also known as closing costs.

Silent Second

An unrecorded second mortgage that is secured by real property.

Simple Interest Mortgage

A mortgage on which interest is paid on a deposit account that is calculated daily based on the balance at the time. This type of loan is not compounded or amortizing.

Stated Assets

A loan program where the verification of the borrower's assets is not required by the lender, but is simply stated on the loan application.

Stated Income

A loan program where the verification of the borrower's income is required by the lender, but is simply stated on the loan application.

Streamlined Refinancing

A refinance that leaves out some of the typical loan requirements/guideline fulfillments. This makes for a quicker and sometime less costly loan.

Subordinate Financing

A second mortgage or a lien that is issued on a property that allows the current first mortgage to be paid off and a new first mortgage to take its place without paying off the current second mortgage or lien. The second mortgage lender must allow subordination of the second to the new first mortgage.

Subordination Policy

The policy of a second mortgage lender that allows a borrower to refinance the first mortgage while not paying off the current second mortgage. The second mortgage retains its original lien position.

Sub-Prime Borrower

A borrower with poor credit or with a loan scenario that is aggressively outside Fannie Mae and Freddie Mac conforming guidelines. This borrower or the loan scenario are considered high-risk and therefore can borrow only from sub-prime lenders who specialize in dealing with borrowers with substandard credit. These borrowers will pay higher interest rates.

Sub-Prime Lender

A lender who specializes in lending to high-risk borrowers, as well as high-risk loans.

Teaser Rate

Also known as the start rate. The initial interest rate the borrower starts out with on an ARM loan, when it is lower than the fully indexed rate.

Temporary Buy-Down

A temporary reduction in the mortgage payment due to paying additional points on the loan. Typically referred to as 3-2-1, meaning the interest rate is three percent lower the first year, two percent lower the second year, and one percent lower the third year.

Term

The period of time used to compute the monthly mortgage payment. The mortgage reaches full maturity when the borrower reaches the end of the term and pays the loan off.

Third Party Fees

The lender charges these fees for services rendered by outside companies. The lender does not keep these fees but adds them as the other companies work on the borrower's files and provide a service to the client.

Title Insurance

Insurance that protects the lender and/or owner against loss in the event of property ownership disputes.

Total Interest Payments

The total of all interest payments over the life of the loan or the total of all interest payments year-to-date.

Truth in Lending (TIL)

The federal law that requires lenders to disclose the truth of what they're lending through a specific form. The information that must be provided to borrowers.

Underwriters

Approve or deny mortgage loans by following mortgage standards and guidelines. They review and evaluate information on mortgage loan documents to determine if buyer, property, and loan conditions meet establishment and government standards. They request additional information from the borrowers for qualification purposes. They assemble documents in loan files, including acceptance or denial, and return files to originating mortgage loan office. They may be authorized by federal agency to certify that mortgage loan applicant and property.

Underwriting

A system of examining the borrower's file to determine whether the mortgage applied for by the borrower should be issued.

VA Mortgage

A mortgage loan approved by a lending institution to U.S. Veterans and is guaranteed by the Veterans Administration. This loan comes with the benefit of no down payment.

VOD

Verification of Deposits. Usually in one's bank account.

VOE

Verification of Employment.

VOM

Verification of Mortgage. To verify that the borrowers have made their mortgage payments consistently.

VOR

Verification of Rent. To verify the prospective borrowers have made their rent payments consistently.

Waive Escrows

When a lender allows the borrowers to pay their taxes and insurance separately from their mortgage payment. The lender waives or allows the borrower to not have to have an escrow account.

Wholesale Lender

A lender who provides loans through mortgage brokers and banks that sell their loans to clients who come through their door.

Yield-Spread Premium (YSP)

An incentive paid by the bank to the broker/loan agent based on the interest rate that is sold to the client. The higher the interest rate, the more yield-spread premium. Yield-Spread Premium is also known as or referred to as "Rebate."

10-03

Pronounced, ten o' three. Another name for the residential loan application a borrower fills out at time of applying for a mortgage loan.